A Bridge Over the Sins of Your Fathers

Was it negligence, deception, or pure evilness, that caused our fathers to hand down to us a corrupted version of Christ's gospel.

Steve Garrett

New Harbor Press

RAPID CITY, SD

Copyright © 2023 by Steve Garrett

All rights reserved. No part of this publication may be reproduced, distributed or transmitted in any form or by any means, without prior written permission.

Hunter/New Harbor Press
1601 Mt.Rushmore Rd, Ste 3288
Rapid City, SD 57701
www.newharborpress.com
A bridge Over the Sins of Your Fathers / Steve Garrett. -- 1st ed.

ISBN 978-1-63357-433-5

Contents

BIBLE REFERENCES 1
WHY THIS BOOK WAS WRITTEN 3
WE ARE NOT ALL ADAM AND EVE'S CHILDREN 13
A MAN DID NOT CAUSE THE FALL OF MANKIND 25
THE NOAHIDE FLOOD WAS A LOCAL EVENT AND
AGAIN, WE ARE STILL NOT ALL BROTHERS 37
ARE GODS OLD TESTAMENT DIETARY LAWS STILL IN
EFFECT? 47
IS THE GAY LIFESTYLE UNACCEPTABLE TO GOD? 61
THE BIBLICAL ROLE FOR WOMEN DEFINED IN GODS
NATURAL ORDER 69
THE TRINITY THAT NEVER WAS 85
IS GOD OMNIPRESENT AND DOES HE KNOW EVERY-
THING ALL THE TIME? 95
REINCARNATION: THE MISSING LINK
IN CHRISTIANITY 105
FLAT EARTH: WHO KNOWS THE STORY? THE CREATOR
OR THE CREATED? 121
THE TRIBULATION IS OVER AND YOU MISSED IT 137
CONCLUSION 171

BIBLE REFERENCES

The NASB (New American Standard Bible) is used for the biblical references in this book. The KJV (King James Version) is noted when it is referenced. I cite non-canonical books when they help bring clarity to biblical issues and stories when the NASB and the KJV are either silent or vague. These non-canonical books I cite are: The Apocrypha. The book of Enoch. The book of Jasher. The Dead Sea Scrolls. The Septuagint. The book of Jubilees. An example of when these books have assisted a bible story is in Exodus when Aaron, the brother of Moses, made the golden calf idol for the tribes of Israel to worship. The bible in Exodus 32: 1 – 4, leaves us believing that Aaron was a willing participant in this rebellious act. But referencing the book of Jasher ch. 82: 12 – 14, we find out that Aaron was forced to make this golden calf under the threat of death. It is stories like these that other non-canonical literature assists the Christian in receiving discernment.

WHY THIS BOOK WAS WRITTEN

APOSTATE: ONE WHO HAS ABANDONED THEIR RELIGIOUS FAITH

It was seven years ago when I began writing this book. At that time there were chapters I was working on back then that today I understand should not be in this book. There are chapters now included that back then I did not have the enlightenment to explain or the revelations to even know about.

It happened one day as I was working on this book. The software in the computer crashed and the only document I lost was this book. I took my computer to two software recovery experts and both threw up their hands and shook their heads. I am sure you can imagine for a long time I was disturbed to the point that I couldn't even restart this book as I pondered the disaster. But as the years went by the good Lord opened up new avenues of understanding for me and I would sometimes catch myself saying, "if I ever write that book again this new revelation would need to be in it."

Finally here I am today blessed with the understanding that the timing of this book needed to be in Gods time and not my own. That

God had not given me the proper discernment back then to properly write this book. So as the timing of this book was not in Gods time back then, I believe the timing of Gods church also was not ready to hear the message of this book back then either.

I used the word "apostasy" to describe the current spiritual state of many churches today. Is my use of this word too strong, too insensitive, or just plain blatantly false? To defend my claim I am going to cite a recent article by Chuck Baldwin. For those who know him no introduction is needed, for those who don't some research of him on your part would be theologically advantageous.

Article: Its official: The American church is apostate. March 4, 2022.

https://www.freedomsphoenix.com/Opinion/320704-2022-02-17-its-official-the-american-church-is-apostate.htm

"I've (Chuck Baldwin) known for many years that the Church in America has fallen to the lowest spiritual state of its entire existence. I've tried to warn Christians in both this column and in my public speaking to the dismal state of today's churches. Researcher George Barna and the Cultural Research Center at Arizona Christian University recently released Barna's latest survey regarding the current state of America's churches and the findings are horrific.

In a poll by the Barna Group, half of those surveyed who described themselves as Christians didn't believe that Satan exists, and one-third were confident that Jesus sinned while he was on earth.

> Also according to the Barna Poll: Today, 176 million Americans claim to be Christians—69% of the population. Yet, only 6% of U.S. adults—which is 9% of those identifying as Christians—possess a biblical worldview, believing the Bible to be accurate and reliable, among other convictions.
>
> Large majorities of self-identified Christians also report many beliefs not in harmony with biblical teaching according to the survey. These include:

* 72% argue that people are basically good.
* 66% say that 'having faith' matters more than which faith you pursue.
* 64% say that all religious faiths are of equal value.
* 58% believe that if a person is good enough, or does enough good things, they can earn their way into Heaven.
* 57% believe in karma.

Of the 176 million Americans who claim to be Christians, only 9% of them believe the Bible to be the true Word of God and thus might genuinely be saved. ("So then faith cometh by hearing, and hearing by the word of God." Romans 10:17) That means the number of truly born-again Christians in America is probably no more than 15 million. This also means that probably less than 10% of the professing Christians attending America's churches are truly saved. Barna is also astute in highlighting the reason for this massive Christian apostasy: The pulpits are not teaching a sound doctrine. So there it is: By and large, America's pastors are not teaching their people sound doctrine. Hence, the blame for this massive apostasy in the U.S. can be laid squarely at the pulpits of America's churches. One would think that the stark reality of the above report would cause America's pastors to reevaluate their emphasis on church growth, discontinue their motivational speaking sermons, stop turning their churches into glorified social clubs, stop avoiding hard sermons and quit being "yes-men" for civil government and end their un-scriptural infatuation with Christian Zionism. It should; but it won't."

The next question on everyones mind should be: Is Chuck Baldwin the only lone voice sounding the clarion call of the apostate church? Running a simple google search will quickly reveal that Mr. Baldwin is far from alone with his describing the apostate condition of today's churches.

America's Apostate Churches!–Jesus-is-Savior.com
Today's evangelical circles are complacently apostate, completely silent regarding the evils plaguing America. It is tragic. All across America ministers are...
thethirdhelix.com/2015/12/27/the-american-church-is-apostate

The American Church is Apostate | The Third Helix
Dec 27, 2015 ... Worse than that, even – through Fideism, the Church actively prevents people from placing their faith in Jesus Christ. Christians are sabotaging...
decisionmagazine.com/todays-apostasy

Today's Apostasy–Decision Magazine
Apr 30, 2019 ... Many Christians and churches today have abandoned their faith and fallen away from the true Gospel of Jesus Christ.
endtimesprophecyreport.com/2014/03/13/american-apostasy-the-end-times-apostate-american-church

American Apostasy: The End Times Apostate American Church
Mar 13, 2014 ... APOSTATE AMERICA: AN END TIMES CHURCH A POWERFUL AMERICAN CHURCH IS RISING UP A Great Falling Away which will Look Like a Great End Times ...
www.gotquestions.org/apostasy.html
renner.org/videos/the-verdict-on-the-apostate-church

The Verdict on the Apostate Church–Rick Renner Ministrie God's verdict upon the rebellious and the apostate Church is clearly stated in the book of Jude. Rick opens the Scriptures on this topic today.

Apostasy in American Churches–Dave Williams Ministries
Feb 17, 2020 ... Apostasy in American Churches ... The Christian Church, including Charismatics, Pentecostals, ... They Are Sitting in Your Church.

www.theamericanconservative.com/dreher/apostate-churches-anglican-catholic-newcastle-amazon-synod

This is just a small sample of what seems to be occupying the minds of the church watchmen today. But should we really be that surprised at today's church apostasy when the bible forewarned us long ago that when this apostate destination was in our ancestors rear view mirror it was only going to be a matter of time when it would not only overtake the unsuspecting Christian of today but also come to control his world view of the church and of the Christian religion itself.

It was Paul in the book of Acts that gave us the warning.

> Acts 20: 29, *I know that after my departure savage wolves will come in among you, not sparing the flock*; 30, *and from among your own selves men will arise, speaking perverse things, to draw away the disciples after them.*

If one will take the time to notice, Paul is not talking to a specific church, or referencing a specific person. This was a blanket general statement to Gods holy church wherever it resided. Paul was informing us apostasy was on the horizon and all will be affected. Then in the book of Jude, the last book in the bible before Revelations we are informed that the damage was accomplished.

> Jude 1: 3, *Beloved, while I was making every effort to write you about our common salvation, I felt the necessity to write to you appealing that you contend earnestly for the faith which was once for all handed down to the saints.* 4, *For certain persons have crept in unnoticed, those who were long beforehand marked out for this condemnation, ungodly persons who turn the grace of our God into licentiousness and deny our only Master and Lord, Jesus Christ.*

Judes conclusion is a message to all Christians yesterday and today that this gospel corruption comes in many forms as many of todays lukewarm Christians seek to follow their own personal version of the bible book they didn't write.

- God tells us women are not to be above the men in His churches, but witness the churches today supporting the female pastors.
- God condemns homosexuality as a sin but just a quick gaze through the churches stained glass windows and you will witness the gay support for not only congregational inclusion of this lifestyle but also the ordaining of gay priests and pastors.
- It was Jesus Himself that said in John 14:6, *I am the way, and the truth, and the life, no one comes to the father but through me.* But referencing Chuck Baldwins article we find the Cultural Research Center reporting that 66% of Christians say that having faith matters more than which faith you pursue, and 64% say that all religious faiths are of equal value.

So as America drowns itself in multi-cultures and multi-religions is it really any wonder how the once powerful Christian nation called America ended up succumbing to apostasy as many of the muzzled 501c3 preachers of state sponsored religion seek to lead their flocks to friendship with the world instead of obedience to God? Can you envision Jesus or His apostles keeping silent on the corruption of the gospel or even on the corruption of their country to ensure their tax exempt status remained in place?

I have found over the years that people who are not serious church goers but still have a belief in God are more accepting of these ideas I have put forth to them. These types of people are not shackled to a preconditioned belief system and usually possess an open mind when it comes to different ideas about Christianity. But the Christian who has spent his life in either one church or one type of denomination of Christianity will find the words in this book unsettling to their long held belief system.

The path of this type of Christian usually starts with him searching for God, Jesus, or the truth, or a combination of the three. He usually will have some sort of mentor or encouragement from family or friends to help guide him on his way. Eventually this Christian reaches a point in their lives where something just clicks and then they feel they have gotten their sought after answer and it is usually in the comfort and security of a Church. It is at this point in his life the Christian feels he has accomplished his goal and is now in his mind – saved. Armed with this understanding he now becomes a defender of his chosen type of faith, be it Baptist, Catholic, Jehovah Witness, or whichever Church it is. But defenders need walls and it is those walls that the Christian has built around himself over the years that keeps him entrenched in a belief system that hinders spiritual development in certain ways. This Christian will argue that he is developing his spirituality within his church but what he usually is doing is defending and developing his previously acquired testimony. You will hear this type of Christian say things like, "we believe this" or "my God is that". "Our Church looks at it this way" or "my pastor doesn't look at it that way." So what I am saying is when this Christian reaches his "aha" moment in life, the next logical task for him to do is to build a wall around this moment as he begins his new life as a defender of his faith.

How do I know this? I was that guy. It was me who used to walk around all smug just knowing I was special because someone in my Church told me I was.

When a Christian from another denomination would try to share his views with me I would confidently smile at the lost individual and when this annoying short sited person finally got through babbling I would unload some reality on them. At least some of the reality I thought I possessed at that time.

It was through youth and marriage that I ended up darkening the doors of Churches in the three prominent Christian denominations.

A Protestant Church, an Orthodox Church, and a Church some consider a cult type of Christian faith. Each claimed in some way to be the true Church and each condemned the other faiths in some way or another. Being a part of these churches at first caused me to feel set apart and unique in my faith, but later in life it just left me confused as I considered the claims of each of the three different faiths. So one day while pondering these three very different Christian theological experiences I picked up the bible and asked God, "will you show me what you think about your book?" And with that question I opened up my mind and my heart to receive Gods direction of wherever He decided He would take me. Since that day God has lead me to the discernment and discoveries that fill the pages of this book.

So as the Watchmen's cry of apostasy in the church reaches fever pitch will the Christian heed the warning? Will the pages of this book bring understanding to the Christian? I would guess its up to each individual as they take their own spiritual journey in life.

What the messages in Acts 20, and Jude 1, should tell us is that the theological corruption of Christs true gospel happened long ago and this same corruption over time has been handed on down to you by your fathers.

The premise of this book is: The word of God was not corrupted. What became corrupted is man's perception of His word.

To pave the way for a rejection of mans inherited corrupt perception of Gods word the Christian must realign his beliefs with Gods truth by opening his mind, opening his heart, and sometimes we just need to do this.

Mark 10: 15, (Jesus) Truly I say to you, whoever does not receive the kingdom of God like a child will not enter it at all.

NOTE: This book uses biblical references from the New American Standard Bible.

The KJV will be noted when that bible is referenced.

CHAPTER ONE

WE ARE NOT ALL ADAM AND EVE'S CHILDREN

For the Christian world to believe that it is from Adam and Eve that every person on earth can retrace their family roots to, one must sign on to the fantasy that two genetically identical people can produce children of the Caucasian race, the Negroid race, the Asian race, and the native Indian race, and everything in between. The scientific fact that there are are no historic records proving that such a union can produce multiracial offspring does not get in the way of today's churches quest to believe the impossible.

The four basic theories to support this view of all people on earth are related by way of Adam and Eve are as follows:

Theory 1: Adam and Eve had special and unique reproductive genes, even though who ever made this claim never knew them personally, and never read it in the bible, but undeterred, some Christians will sign onto this thinking because nothing else makes sense to them.

Theory 2: God created the different races after the judgment of the Tower of Babel when he separated the people and changed their languages. Now never mind that God never made such a claim but inserting this new idea helps this type of Christian explain their chosen narrative.

Theory 3: The races were created by their environment. Hence the closer one lived to the equator the darker their skin became due to the exposure to increased sunlight. I guess in the believers mind this same sun was able to genetically influence the color of their hair and eyes also.

Theory 4: The Process of Micro-Evolution, which can be natural or God might have influenced, or perhaps a combination of both. This process influenced the genetic development of different genetic traits among humans over thousands of years. To me the use of words such as "might" and "perhaps" are not the words confident people use to describe ideas they think you should believe in.

NOTE: An exception must be noted. It has been documented that the intercourse of an interracial couple can genetically influence a child a few generations removed. Since Adam and Eve were genetically the same this exception does not apply to them.

Lets also not forget the theological pole vaulting backwards some Christians do when they explain that when man was created in Gen. 1: 27, the bible was really talking about Adam, even though Adam wasn't mentioned in the bible till Genesis 2. This bible timeline rearranging must have come from an authority these Christians seem to have personally given to themselves because I never read in the bible that its readers can change the book anytime they see the need or get confused.

Taking these ideas into consideration it seems history and reality keep getting in the way of these very creative unproven theories. So how does one scientifically approach this bizarre christian claim of Adam and Eve were the first inhabitants of Gods earth and produced racially different offspring when genetic science and secular history has been a constant reminder that the opposite is actually the truth? Since the Christian rejects science and history I recommend searching for a biblical answer.

The bible as we know is a history recorded sequentially in basically a linear timeline order. With this understanding we will consider the concept of pre-Adamic man. It was God who created "man and woman" in Genesis 1.

> Gen. 1: 27, *God created man in His own image, in the image of God He created him; male and female He created them.*

There is no mention of any guy named Adam in verse 27. That event arrives in Gen. 2: 7. So what this means is there is an undeniable scriptural time separation of these two events of mans creation and Adams arrival. Its what happens between these two recorded events that will bring clarity to this issue. After man and woman were created God acknowledged that all He created was good and let us know the last day of His work of creation was the 6th day.

> Gen. 2: 1, *Thus the heavens and the earth were completed, and all their hosts. 2, By the seventh day God completed His work which He had done, and He rested on the seventh day from all His work which He had done. 3, Then God blessed the seventh day and sanctified it, because in it He rested from all His work which God had created and made.*

So the Christian has been officially informed in Gen. 2, that the creation process by God is over and no mention of Adam yet.

In Gen. 2: verse 4, with the creation process over the bible is now referencing an "undocumented" historical timeline. A lot is being said in this verse without actually saying it.

> NASB Gen. 2: 4, *This is **the account** of the heavens and the earth **when** they **were** created, in the day that the LORD God **made** earth and heaven.*

> KJV Gen. 2: 4, ***These are the generations*** *of the heavens and of the earth **when** they **were** created, in the day that the LORD God **made** the earth and the heavens.*

The language used in both the NASB and the KJV is telling us that 1) a **past historic creation event** is being referenced by God, and 2) that **an undocumented amount of time has passed.** So with the addition of verse 4, we have a coherent precise timeline referenced in the bible with no personal additions, narrative insertions, or rearranged timelines.

> Gen. 1: 27, Man and Woman were created.
> Gen. 1: 31, God finished the creation process on the 6th day.
> Gen. 2: 3, On the 7th day God rested.
> Gen. 2: 4, An undocumented amount of time has passed (generations) long enough to make an (account) of a timeline in past tense terms, and still no mention of Adam yet.

What we are witnessing is an undocumented gap of time that is referenced in verses 4 thru 6, that leaves us wondering what was going on during those generations between the creation of man and the arrival of Adam.

2: 4, This is the account of the heavens and the earth when they were created, in the day that the LORD God made earth and heaven. 5, Now no shrub of the field was yet in the earth, and no plant of the field had yet sprouted, for the LORD God had not sent rain upon the earth, and there was no man to cultivate the ground. 6, But a mist used to rise from the earth and water the whole surface of the ground.

This brings us to what some people believe is called the "Gap Theory". In a nutshell this theory says God created the heavens and earth in Gen. 1:1. Then there was a long undocumented time span after verse 1. But in verse 2, God destroyed the earth and then began the re-creation process of the earth a 2nd time in verse 3, which then took 6 days.

My take on the Gap Theory moves the undocumented timeline from Gen. 1. 1, to Gen.2: 4 through verse 6.

Witness in Gen. 2: 4, the undocumented timeline is referenced, but then the story takes an abrupt U-turn in the very next verse.

> Gen. 2: 5, ***"Now"*** *no shrub of the field was yet in the earth, and no plant of the field had yet **sprouted**, for the LORD God had not sent rain upon the earth, and there was no man to cultivate the ground. 6, But a mist used to rise from the earth and water the whole surface of the ground.*

This verse is claiming that something on the earth has dramatically changed because **"Now"** plants aren't growing and its because God stopped sending rain upon the earth. Notice the phrase: a mist "used to" rise from the earth. Past tense.

During this undocumented timeline God stopped watering the earth with rain and a mist "used to" (past tense) water the earth during that time. The reason we know something on the earth has changed is because there were waters in the heavens for rain created by God in Gen. 1.

> Gen. 1: 6, *Then God said, "Let there be an expanse in the midst of the waters, and let it separate the waters from the waters." 7, God made the expanse, and separated the **waters which were below the expanse from the waters which were above the expanse;** and it was so.*

And we also were told that plants and trees were also bearing fruit back in Gen. 1.

> Gen. 1: 11, *Then God said, "Let the earth **sprout** vegetation, plants yielding seed, and fruit trees on the earth bearing fruit after their kind with seed in them";* **and it was so.** 11, **The earth brought forth vegetation, plants** *yielding seed after*

their kind, and trees bearing fruit with seed in them, after their kind; and God saw that it was good.

Adding to the story God tells us in Gen. 2: 5, *there was no man to till (or cultivate) the ground.* This statement could be explained in a few ways.

1. There never needed to be a farmer type of person for feeding people during the time frame of Gen.1: 27, to Gen. 2: 3.
2. There used to be farmers during that same time frame but during some cataclysmic event man lost the knowledge and/or ability to grow food for his preservation.
3. *No man to cultivate the ground,* could be a metaphor for no man to start multiplying his seed/offspring on the earth i.e. like a garden.

Whatever the explanation is, God lets us know something happened during this gap period between Gen. 4 thru 6, that made Him claim that the plants "now" didn't grow, and that He did not bring rain on the earth, and there was "now" not a man to "cultivate" the land.

So what the good book is telling us is the earth was fully functioning with plants, rain, animals, and man, by the time God had completed his creation in Gen. 2:3. **But somewhere in-between verses Gen. 2: 4, and verse 6,** some unexplainable and unrecorded event occurred and Gods reaction was to stop sending rain and one of the results of His action caused the earths plants to stop growing.

And there is your Gap.

By Gen. 2:7 God is now in repair mode for the earth and hence, the arrival of Adam.

> Gen. 2:7, *Then the LORD God formed man of dust from the ground, and breathed into his nostrils the breath of life; and man became a living being.*

A re-starting point. God forms this guy named Adam and plants a garden giving us the understanding that things are going to get back to at least a form of normal. But looking a little closer we find the arrival of Adam is described differently from the creation of man in Gen. 1: 27.

Creation of man:

> Gen. 1: 27, *God created man in His own image, in the image of God He created him; male and female He created them.*

Formation of Adam:
> KJV: **Gen. 2: 7,** *And the LORD God formed man of the dust of the ground, and breathed into his nostrils the breath of life; and* **man became a living soul**.

> NASB: **Gen. 2: 7,** *Then the LORD God formed man of dust from the ground, and breathed into his nostrils the breath of life; and* **man became a living being**.

The only difference between the KJV version and the NASB version are the two words:
Living **soul.**
Living **being.**

Living Soul and Living Being are listed in Strong's Concordance under the number: 5315. Both of these two word phrases in the NASB and KJV are listed under the same word. Nephesh 5315. A living Being is also a Living Soul.

For the first time in the bible, the word "soul" is used to describe someone. A new type of being unlike all others. You will note God did not say He created Adam. The word He used was "formed." To form, does not mean to create. To use an analogy, the clay must be created before it can be formed. What I am saying is Adam was already alive before God genetically modified (formed) him to receive a soul. Now here is where the modern Christian will claim the words "form" and "create" mean the same thing.

Merriam-Webster dictionary:
Create: To bring into existence.
Form: To give a particular shape to something; To shape or mold into a certain state.

The definition of these two words are nothing of the same.

Or, the Christian will say the bible just used the word "form" to mean "create".

Not true. The writer of Genesis knew the difference between these two words and uses the word "create" no less than four times in Genesis 1, showing us that the bibles use of the word "form" was a choice and definitive of the action performed in Gen. 2: 7. So with the application of the word "form" when referring to Adams arrival in the Garden of Eden we are led to believe God genetically modified a pre-Garden of Eden man (Adam) into a man with a soul. Where Adam was before receiving his soul the bible leaves us in the dark until after the fall of man had occurred.

> Gen. 3: 23, *therefore the LORD God sent him* (Adam) *out from the garden of Eden, to cultivate the ground **from which he was taken.***

In verse 23, the bible tells us Adam was sent "back" to the place that he was taken from prior to his arrival in the Garden of Eden validating the claim that Adam was not created just before being placed in the Garden of Eden. Adam was actually living life as a man at another place on earth before receiving his soul. So what we have uncovered so far is this timeline:

1. God creates the heavens and earth.
2. God creates man and woman **and commanded them to be fruitful and multiply and fill the earth.**

3. An undocumented timeline gap happened generations after the creation of all things.
4. Adam is brought in from a place where he was living and then genetically modified by God (formed) into a man with a soul.

Referencing timeline point 2, we see–Gen. 1: 28, *God blessed them; and God said to them, "Be fruitful and multiply, and fill the earth, and subdue it; and rule over the fish of the sea and over the birds of the sky and over every living thing that moves on the earth.*

So we can safely assume these men and women obeyed Gods commandment in Gen. 1, and multiplied over the earth and living among them at some point in time was Adam, but not Eve. Was Adam the first man ever to be created in Gen. 1: 27? The bible does not name him to be. But what we are told is many generations of people lived on the earth before Adam received his soul and then was placed in the Garden of Eden. Was there other people besides Adam living with him on earth after the (cataclysmic?) event of the undocumented timeline (gap) and during the time he received his soul? The bible tells us there was.

After the genetic modification of Adam we witness the arrival of Eve, his helpmeet.

> Gen. 2: 18, *Then the LORD God said, "It is not good for the man to be alone; I will make him a helper suitable for him.*

> Gen. 2: 20, *The man gave names to all the cattle, and to the birds of the sky, and to every beast of the field, but for Adam* ***there was not found a helper suitable for him.***

> 21, *So the LORD God caused a deep sleep to fall upon the man, and he slept; then He took one of his ribs and closed up the flesh at that place.*

> 22, *The LORD God **fashioned** into a woman the rib which He had taken from the man, and brought her to the man.*

Notice the words "formed" or "created" were not used to describe the arrival of Eve, but "fashioned". This word perfectly describes how Eve was brought into the world. What this fashioning of Eve from Adams rib did was create a perfect genetic match for Adam who was already genetically modified to receive a soul. Now I want to draw your attention back to verse 20.

20, *...but for Adam there was not found a helper suitable for him.*

What this verse is telling us is there was a search for a mate for Adam and none was found suitable for him. That tells us that there were known females living in the world and God knew they were out there, but after conducting a search and checking out who was available, none of these women were judged to be a proper wife for Adam. So it was after this search was conducted that God proceeded to create Eve. This should tell the discerning Christian that:

1. There were women living in the world before Eve arrived.
2. There were people living in the world before Eve arrived.

It was these other people who were known to be alive at that time that Eve's son, Cain was referencing when he said to God:

> Gen. 4: 14, *Behold, You have driven me this day from the face of the ground; and from Your face I will be hidden, and I will be a vagrant and a wanderer on the earth, and **whoever finds me will kill me.***

At this point does God tell Cain, "are you crazy? With Abel gone its now only you and Adam and Eve who are left alive on earth." Not hardly and not really. What God does do is validate Cain's claim that other unnamed people are out there.

> **Gen. 4: 15,** *So the LORD said to him, "Therefore whoever kills Cain, vengeance will be taken on him sevenfold." And the LORD appointed a sign for Cain, so that no one finding him would slay him.*

God says "whoever" when referencing who might kill Cain thus letting us know there was enough unnamed people out there to cause Cain to have concern for his life.

But no mention in this verse of Adam or Eve being the whoever. NOTE: Now some say Cain got his wife from a future daughter of Adam and Eve. This is actually documented in the ancient non-canonical book of Jubilees:

> **Jubilees: Ch. 4: 9,** *And Cain took Awan his sister to be his wife and she bare him Enoch.*

So taking all points into account when considering the claim that we here on earth are all not Adam and Eves children:

1. We have the bible telling us Adam was alive and well among the other people that multiplied on the earth before he was brought into the garden of Eden.
2. We understand many generations of man had passed before an undocumented gap (cataclysmic?) event happened.
3. After Adam was given a soul and placed in the Garden of Eden we have God searching for a suitable mate for Adam among the women in the land/earth and finding none suitable for Adam before Eve ever came to be.
4. We have Cain fearing for his life because of the other people that were alive in the land who might hold a grudge against him for killing Abel.
5. Lastly we have God himself validating Cain's claim of those other people that indeed were alive in the land during that time.

So the bible is clear that the world was and still is not populated with people that can all trace their lineage back to Adam and Eve. That Adam and Eve created a bloodline that carried a soul that was separate from the other bloodlines on the earth at that time. And that bloodline started with Seth and can be traced all the way to Jesus Himself as documented in Luke 3.

CHAPTER TWO

A MAN DID NOT CAUSE THE FALL OF MANKIND

For a rational person to actually believe that something as historically and biblically devastating as the fall of mankind was caused by eating an apple is silly at best. To believe that the God of all creation, wiser than all, more powerful than all, would be so bothered by a missing piece of low hanging fruit from a tree just doesn't seem to square with the deeds of a God as magnificent as the one described in the bible. I understand Eve was tempted and beguiled by the serpent. I understand to God himself this act was an act of rebellion. But to myself, the consequences inflicted upon the world at that time and for all time yet to come just seems a little over played for the sake of one piece of fruit.

As bible believers we know the good book uses metaphors to explain issues and stories so can we assume that just maybe there might be some of those same metaphors in this story concerning the fall of man?

> Gen. 3: 1-4, *Now the serpent was more crafty than any beast of the field which the LORD God had made. And he said to the woman, "Indeed, has God said, 'You shall not eat from any tree of the garden'?"* 2, *The woman said to the serpent, "From the fruit of the trees of the garden we may eat;* 3, *but from the fruit of the tree which is in the middle of the garden,*

> *God has said, 'You shall not eat from it or touch it, or you will die. 4, The serpent said to the woman, "You surely will not die!*

This serpent is none other than Satan himself because verse 1, tells us this serpent was *"more crafty than all the other beasts God had made"* and in Revelations this same serpent is identified as Satan twice.

> Rev. 12: 9, *And the great dragon was thrown down, the **serpent** of old who is called the devil and **Satan**, who deceives the whole world; he was thrown down to the earth, and his angels were thrown down with him.*

> Rev. 2-0: 2, *And he laid hold of the dragon, the **serpent** of old, who is the devil and **Satan**, and bound him for a thousand years.*

So we have one player in the Garden of Eden identified as Satan, but another player is still out there.

> Gen. 2: 9, *Out of the ground the LORD God caused to grow every tree that is pleasing to the sight and good for food; the tree of life also in the midst of the garden, and the **tree of the knowledge of good and evil**.*

Looking at this verse we see that God said "every tree was pleasing to look at and good for food" then we have an abrupt stop in the sentence and God then says there are also two other trees in the garden.

1. Tree of Life
2. Tree of the knowledge of good and evil.

We notice that these two trees are separated in Gods statement from the other trees that are good for food. God says nothing about these two trees being good for food but just says that they are there.

So tell me. What does a tree of life look like? What does a tree of knowledge of good and evil look like? Are these trees metaphors?

> Gen. 3: 4, *The serpent said to the woman, "You surely will not die! 5, For God knows that in the day you eat from it your eyes will be opened, and you will be like God, knowing good and evil.*

Here we have a contradiction. Eve and the serpent are talking about **eating** from the **tree** that was in the "midst" of the garden that God never said was good for food. So we are starting to see that there are two words in this story that could be judged as out of place and just maybe used as a metaphor.

1. Tree
2. Eat

At this point we need to ask ourselves has the bible used the word "tree" as a metaphor in other bible verses?

> Judges 9: 8, *Once **the trees** went forth to anoint a king over them, and **they said** to the olive tree, '**Reign over us!**' 9, But the olive tree said to them, 'Shall I leave my fatness with which God and men are honored, and go to wave over the trees?' 10, Then the trees said to the fig tree, 'You come, reign over us!' 11, But the fig tree said to them, 'Shall I leave my sweetness and my good fruit, and go to wave over the trees?' 12, Then the trees said to the vine, 'You come, reign over us*

> 1 Chron. 16: 33, *Then the **trees** of the forest will **sing for joy** before the LORD; For He is coming to judge the earth.*

> Isaiah 55: 12, *For you will go out with joy, And be led forth with peace; The mountains and the hills will break forth into shouts of joy before you, And all the **trees** of the field will **clap their hands**.*

> Proverbs 3: 13, *How blessed is the man who finds **wisdom**, And the man who gains understanding.*

After verse 13 and skip to verse 18, *She **(wisdom)** is a **tree** of life to those who take hold of her, And happy are all who hold her **(wisdom)** fast.*

> Psalms 37: 35, *I have seen a **wicked**, violent man, Spreading himself like a luxuriant **tree** in its native soil.*

Doing a search we find the bible does use the word "tree" as a metaphor for several things.

1. Trees can talk
2. Tree have feelings
3. Trees have human physical characteristics.
4. Trees have wisdom
5. Trees are wicked.

Putting all these listed metaphors of trees together we can fashion a type of being that can talk, has feelings, has human physical characteristics, is wise, but is also wicked. So can we look at this tree of knowledge in Gen. 2: 9, as a metaphor for something else? How about a metaphor for a fallen angel? Moving sideways and into the book of Enoch you will find that this tree of knowledge that was in the Garden of Eden has a name.

> Enoch 69: 6, *And the third (chief of the fallen angels) was named Gadreel, he it is who showed the children of men all the blows of death, **and he led astray Eve**, and showed weapons of death to the sons of men, the shield, coat of mail, and the sword for battle, and all the weapons of death to the children of men. 7. And from his hand they have proceeded against those who dwell on the earth from that day and evermore.*

This 3rd Chief of the fallen ones, Gadreel did two wicked things.

1. Introduced the sons of men to war and the weapons of war.
2. Led Eve astray.

NOTE: Gadreel is not called or identified as a serpent as Satan is, so he is not to be confused with the serpent in the Garden of Eden. He is the one who is described in a metaphor as the tree of knowledge of good and evil. He is third chief of Satan's army in the midst of the garden taking orders from Satan to do his bidding. It is he who led Eve astray to sin.

How does Eve describe Gadreel (the tree of knowledge).

> Gen. 3: 6, *When the woman saw that the tree was good for food, and that it was a delight to the eyes, and that the tree was desirable to make* one *wise, she took from its fruit and ate; and she gave also to her husband with her, and he ate.*

Does Eve sound like she is describing a tree or just maybe something else like a desirable man?

1. It was a delight to her eyes.
2. It was desirable.
3. It would make her wise.

So if we now understand that this tree of knowledge of good and evil is not a real tree but a metaphor for a chief of Satans angels, let us consider the second out of place word that could also be a metaphor. "Eat."

> Proverbs 30: 20, *This is the way of an adulterous woman: She **eats** and wipes her mouth, And says, "I have done no wrong."*

I have found one related metaphor of "eat" in Proverbs, but it is clear and concise as it needs to be. Verse 20, is not telling us an adulterous woman eats apples and says I didn't do anything wrong. This verse is talking about adultery not lunch. Just replace the word "eats" with "has adulterous sex" and this metaphor brings a clear understanding to this verse. What we are seeing is the word "eat" is also used as a metaphor in the bible to also mean "have sex".

So the real story here is Satan coaxed Eve into disobeying Gods commandment to stay away from Gadreel (i.e. the tree of knowledge of good and evil). Eve then had sex with Gadreel and then at some later point in time coaxed Adam into having sex with her and that is why they found out they were both naked. But didn't God also warn Adam also not to take of the fruit of Gadreel i.e. tree of knowledge?

> Gen. 2: 16, *The LORD God commanded the man, saying, "From any tree of the garden you may eat freely; 17, but from the tree of the knowledge of good and evil you shall not eat, for in the day that you eat from it you will surely die."*

Was God telling Adam not to have a homosexual relationship with Gadreel? Was this fallen angel capable of having homosexual sex? Our answer is found in the bible book of Jude.

> Jude 1: 6, *And **angels who did not keep their own domain**, but abandoned their proper abode, He has kept in eternal bonds under darkness for the judgment of the great day, 7, **just as Sodom and Gomorrah** and the cities around them, **since they in the same way as these indulged in gross immorality and went after strange flesh**, are exhibited as an example in undergoing the punishment of eternal fire.*

So it is clear God warned both Adam and Eve to stay clear of Gadreel because of the sinful sex involved. In the book of Enoch, Gadreel is described as a male and thus this unlawful sexual union between him and Eve produced an heir and his name was Cain.

> Gen. 3: 16, *To the woman He said, "I will greatly multiply Your pain in childbirth, In pain you will bring forth children....*

It is clear that the Lord knows whats coming and informs Eve she will be expecting.

> Gen. 4: 1, *Now the man had relations with his wife Eve, and she conceived and gave birth to Cain, and she said,* "**I have gotten a manchild with the help of the LORD.**"

Here we are told Adam is having marital relations with his wife and she conceives and gives birth to Cain, but who is Eve naming as the father? Eve specifically says she birthed Cain not with the help of Adam but with the help of a **Lord,** Gadreel, her first sexual encounter.

This Lord, meaning not God the father, but a Lord type of being.

> Gen. 3: 5, *For God knows that in the day you eat from it your eyes will be opened, and* **you will be like "God"** *knowing good and evil.*

The type of God/Lord, Satan is describing is (Gadreel) who knew the difference between good and evil" that the serpent said Eve would be like if she took of the forbidden fruit. It is this Lord that Eve gives credit to for helping her birth Cain.

And next we find out that Man has Fallen.

> Gen. 3: 15, *And* **I will put enmity Between you and the woman, And between your seed and her seed;** *He shall bruise you on the head, And you shall bruise him on the heel.*"

Merriam Webster Dictionary: Enmity – A positive, active, mutual hatred.

It wasn't a fruit snack before lunch that caused the Lord to place an everlasting hatred between the seed of Adam (and Eve) and the seed of Gadreel (and Eve) thus bringing about the fall of mankind.

It was the mixing of the holy (soul) blood line of Adam and Eve with the bloodline of a satanic fallen angel. Now Satan through the sexual union of Gadreel and Eve had planted a new bloodline on the

earth. One that was half Adamic and half Satanic and his name was Cain. And a war was now on the horizon that would span the generations of children to come. A holy conflict of the ages that still rages on today. From a world of peace in the Garden of Eden to a world of never ending hatred and war.
Witness: The fall of Man.

With the true heir of Adam and Eve, Abel, murdered by his half brother, Eve, later in scripture again lets us know with the arrival of Seth that Cain was not Adams son.

> Gen. 4: 25, *Adam had relations with his wife again; and she gave birth to a son, and named him Seth, for,* she said, *"God has appointed me **another offspring in place of Abel**, for Cain killed him.*

Here Eve is clearly admitting Cain who was still alive was not the bloodline replacement for Abel because he was from Gadreels bloodline and not from Adams.

It was God who also had no regard for Cains offering of his fruit from the ground because he was not the rightful heir of Adam.

> Gen. 4: 4, *Abel, on his part also brought of the firstlings of his flock and of their portions. And the LORD had regard for Abel and for his offering;* 5, *but for Cain and for his offering He had no regard. So Cain became very angry and his countenance fell.*

Does the question of Cains bloodline arise in how two genetically perfect human beings with a soul could produce a cold blooded murderer for a son that could look God Himself in the face and lie to Him? If we zoom forward to Luke 3, we find one bible name missing from Adams lineage.

> Luke 3: 23, *When He began His ministry, Jesus Himself was about thirty years of age, being, as was supposed, the son of*

Joseph, the son of Eli, 24, the son of Matthat, the son of Levi, the son of Melchi, the son of Jannai, the son of Joseph, 25, the son of Mattathias, the son of Amos, the son of Nahum, the son of Hesli, the son of Naggai, 26, he son of Maath, the son of Mattathias, the son of Semein, the son of Josech, the son of Joda, 27, the son of Joanan, the son of Rhesa, the son of Zerubbabel, the son of Shealtiel, the son of Neri, 28, the son of Melchi, the son of Addi, the son of Cosam, the son of Elmadam, the son of Er, 29, the son of Joshua, the son of Eliezer, the son of Jorim, the son of Matthat, the son of Levi, 30, the son of Simeon, the son of Judah, the son of Joseph, the son of Jonam, the son of Eliakim, 31, the son of Melea, the son of Menna, the son of Mattatha, the son of Nathan, the son of David, 32, the son of Jesse, the son of Obed, the son of Boaz, the son of Salmon, the son of Nahshon, 33, the son of Amminadab, the son of Admin, the son of Ram, the son of Hezron, the son of Perez, the son of Judah, 34, the son of Jacob, the son of Isaac, the son of Abraham, the son of Terah, the son of Nahor, 35, the son of Serug, the son of Reu, the son of Peleg, the son of Heber, the son of Shelah, 36, the son of Cainan, the son of Arphaxad, the son of Shem, the son of Noah, the son of Lamech, 37, the son of Methuselah, the son of Enoch, the son of Jared, the son of Mahalaleel, the son of Cainan, 38, the son of Enosh, **the son of Seth, the son of Adam, the son of God.**

Again, no mention of Cain being in Adams (or Christs) bloodline. You will also note Abel is not mentioned because he was killed by Cain before he had offspring.

I fully understand in today's Hollywood popular culture the need to blame man for everything but considering the events that led up to the Fall of Man the blame actually rests on a womans shoulders and that woman would be Eve. Following the Garden of Eden story we know that Eve:

1. Was properly warned by God NOT to take of the forbidden fruit from the tree of knowledge (Gadreel).
2. She was not forced by the Serpent to take of the fruit.
3. She fully admits she was deceived by the serpent to disobey Gods commandment.
4. And she also admits she did break Gods commandment and did do the deed.

It was Eve who listened to Satan (the serpent) and let herself be deceived by her curiosity and lustful desires full knowing she was breaking Gods commandment and then exercising her free will she (who was not under the authority of Adam at that time) had sex with Gadreel, aka the tree of knowledge of good and evil. After her sexual encounter with Gadreel, she convinced Adam to join in her sin. We do not know how much time elapsed between her intercourse with Gadreel and her giving sex to her husband Adam, we only know it happened in this order.

When God found out what happened in the Garden of Eden He doles out their punishments in the order they were committed.

> **(First: the serpent)** Gen. 3: 14, *Because you have done this, Cursed are you more than all cattle, And more than every beast of the field; On your belly you will go, And dust you will eat All the days of your life; 15, And I will put enmity Between you and the woman, And between your seed and her seed; He shall bruise you on the head, And you shall bruise him on the heel."*

> **(Second: the woman–Eve)** Gen. 3: 13, *Then the LORD God said to the woman, "What is this you have done?"*

Eve then fully admits that it was her who partook of the forbidden fruit of knowledge. Then God doles out the next punishment to her.

Gen. 3: 16, *To the woman He said, "I will greatly multiply Your pain in childbirth, In pain you will bring forth children; Yet your desire will be for your husband, And he will rule over you."*

(**Third**: **Adam**) Gen. 3: 17, *Then to Adam He said, "**Because you have listened to the voice of your wife**, and have eaten from the tree* (Metaphor: for had sex with Eve) *about which I commanded you, saying, 'You shall not eat from it';Cursed is the ground because of you; In toil you will eat of it All the days of your life.....*

So we have the three punishments in order:

1. The serpent was cursed by God because he deceived Eve.
2. Eve was cursed by God because it was she who disobeyed God commandment to NOT take of the fruit of the tree of knowledge of good and evil. (Gadreel)
3. Adam was cursed because he listened to Eve.

Adam was not deceived by the serpent. Adam did not break Gods commandment with regards to staying away from the tree of knowledge. Eve did that all by herself. But witness today many Christian women (and men) scoffing at Gods natural order and the womans place in it. Eve earned her place in Gods natural order by her own free will actions to have her husband put in the leadership role in the marriage between man and woman for all time. From her sin came the Fall of Man and the introduction of Gods natural order of the family and yes this is also New Testament Scripture.

1 Corrinthians, 11: *But I want you to understand that Christ is the head of every man, and the man is the head of a woman, and God is the head of Christ.*

1 Timothy, 2: 11, *A woman must quietly receive instruction with entire submissiveness.* 12, *But I do not allow a woman to teach or exercise authority over a man, but to remain quiet.* 13, *For it was Adam who was first created,* and *then Eve* 14, **And it was not Adam who was deceived, but the woman being deceived, fell into transgression**. 15, But women *will be preserved through the bearing of children if they continue in faith and love and sanctity with self-restraint.*

So as the war of the ages rages on in the world of today as it will continue with the children of tomorrow, the bible is clear and true. It was Eve, the woman who caused the Fall of Mankind.

CHAPTER THREE

THE NOAHIDE FLOOD WAS A LOCAL EVENT AND AGAIN, WE ARE STILL NOT ALL BROTHERS

The question for the Christian is; was the Flood of Noah worldwide or rather a local event? I myself have brought this question up in certain circles and more than a few times I hear the response. "Seashells have been found on a mountain". I guess we are not allowed to think someone could have actually had the ability to take them there at some point in history. While myself a serious bible believer, I find there is no good reason I can think of that tells me a flood did not happen during Noah's time. God Himself said this story happened and to me that settles it. The question is how big was it? I am not here to scientifically argue about how much water it would take to cover the world or discuss ancient archaeological land masses and their underground wells. I will be quoting the bible and other non-canonical sources to prove that the flood as spoken of by Noah was more of a local flood and therefore other races in other geographical locations were not affected by this event.

Question: Did God actually tell us the flood was worldwide? Consider the original biblical Hebrew word used to describe the land mass that the flood was told to have taken place on.

Erets (Eretz) Strongs Concordance #776.

1. Earth 2. Land (prime root definitions)

But in Strongs Concordance this word "erets" also could have meant, Countries, Countries and their lands, Countryside, Distance, Dust, Ground, Plateau, Region, Territories, World, and Soil.

So what we have here is some individual(s) before our current time made a conscious decision to choose one of the prime root definitions of the Hebrew word "erets" over the other to describe the flood. This someone chose for the bible that Noah's flood was worldwide by sliding just one small step sideways in this words 2 prime root definitions and selected – Earth, instead of – Land. So what could have been described as land in Noah's flood story, was chosen to be earth, by nothing more than someones selected choice.

The next question that arises to the thinking persons mind is how did four guys travel the entire earth catching rhinoceros's, lions, and even chasing down a 75 mph running cheetah and his chick, and then gather enough food for all these animals for 150 days while at the same time build a boat big enough to house them all?

The typical answer from the Christian is "well its obvious God made this happen for Noah by making the animals cooperate with him". Why God just told them to march peacefully in that ark two by two just like in the movies right? Never mind that in the real world the lions would have munched half the animals while standing in line. But is this claim by the believing Christian that God assisted Noah true? Gen. 6 tells me its not.

Question 1: Who built the Ark?

Gen. 6: 14, (God commands) ***Make for yourself*** *an ark of gopher wood;* ***you shall make*** *the ark with rooms, and shall*

> *cover it inside and out with pitch.* 15, **This is how you shall make it**: *the length of the ark three hundred cubits, its breadth fifty cubits, and its height thirty cubits.* 16, **You shall make a window** *for the ark, and finish it to a cubit from the top; and set the door of the ark in the side of it;* **you shall make it** *with lower, second, and third decks.*

Seems God is not only leaving all the work to Noah but also telling him how to build this ark. No less than 5 times in this listed scripture God tells Noah that it is he who is responsible for building the ark. God is repetitively clear about just "WHO" is going to do all the work.

Question 2: Who gathered all the animals?

> Gen. 6: 19, *And of every living thing of all flesh,* **you shall bring** *two of every* kind *into the ark, to keep* them *alive with you; they shall be male and female.* 20, *Of the birds after their kind, and of the animals after their kind, of every creeping thing of the ground after its kind, two of every* kind *will come to you to keep* them *alive.*

Again God is clear. "You (Noah) shall bring two of every kind into the ark". God did not say He was going to wave His hand and all the worlds animals were going to peacefully line up and saunter into the Ark two by two did He?

Question 3: Who was going to feed these animals?

> Gen. 6: 21, **As for you, take for yourself** *some of all food which is edible, and* **gather it to yourself**; *and it shall be for food for you* **and for them**.

And yet again all the work fell on Noah and his offsprings shoulders. The bible is clear. God commanded Noah to do all the work of preparing for the coming flood.

Question 4: Did Noah do the job God gave him?

> Gen. 6: 22, *Thus Noah did; according to all that God had commanded him, so he did.*
> Gen. 7: 5, *Noah did according to all that the LORD had commanded him.*

So can I as a bible reader believe that God told Noah (and his sons) to not only build the ark, herd the animals into it, but also to secure food for his family and all the animals? Does not the bible say that Noah had accomplished the task? Does the bible mention anywhere that Noah received help from the Lord? The answer to that question is flat out no. Did Noah thank the Lord for His help anywhere in this story? Again, no.

Since the bible is clear that it was only Noah and his sons that did all the work, is this why this story is too fantastic to believe? Is this why the Christian inserts in his mind the thought that God helped Noah with the ark as He also convinced the animals to line up and walk in it two by two, even though this idea is not scripturally biblical?

Let us just imagine for a moment that the original translators of the bible had selected the other choice of the 2 prime root definitions of the Hebrew word "erets" which was "land" and insert that same word into the story of the flood of Noah.

> *"God commands Noah to build an ark to house his family and the local clean animals and some local unclean animals. Noah and his sons build the ark and herd their clean animals of sheep, cows, and chickens, and their unclean animals of dogs, cats, and horses into the ark. They secure enough food for themselves and their animals. The flood comes and covers the local land by 15 cubits of water and the ark floats for 150 days. With the evil local population destroyed and the waters receded, Noah and his family leave the ark with both clean animals and unclean animals to sustain them in resettling the land."*

Now considering the flood local, does Gods commandments for Noah to accomplish this task of building a boat and collecting local animals seem reasonable and doable for 4 guys? When we use the Hebrew word "erets" for land, this story now doesn't need magic, a vivid imagination, inserted additions to the story, or invented divine intervention from God. It just makes the story real. Noah and his family survived a local flood. Other people/races in other lands were not affected by this local flood and they survived it by reason of geography and their future ancestors are living in this day and age today.

The next question to consider for those who still believe the entire world was covered by water and all the worlds population had drowned is; where did all the worlds different races come from? Did Noah and his kids have those same special genes said to have belonged to Adam and Eve that Christians claim could produce multiracial children?

> NASB Gen. 6: 9, *These are* the records of *the **generations** of Noah. Noah was a righteous man, blameless in his time; Noah walked with God.*
>
> KJV Gen. 6: 9, *These are the **generations** of Noah: Noah was a just man and perfect in his generations, and Noah walked with God.*

So we are getting a pretty good idea God was impressed with Noah and his ancestral lineage as it was reported to be perfect and blameless.

Merriam-Webster dictionary: **Generations**
1. a body of living beings constituting a single step in the line of decent from an ancestor.

In the very next verse we are told Noah is a father. (Gen. 6: 10, *Noah became the father of three sons: Shem, Ham, and Japheth*) So it isn't a far reach to believe that after Noah had his children he was still perfect in his generations and blameless before God. So why was God making an issue out of Noah's ancestral lineage i.e. generations?

> Gen. 6: 12, *God looked on the earth, and behold, it was corrupt; for all flesh had corrupted their way upon the earth.* (or upon the **land**)

Here God is telling us that all flesh (human type of life) was corrupted i.e. not the way God had originally created it. What was this flesh corruption? Taking a few steps backward we in find verse 2.

> Gen. 6: 2, *that the sons of God saw that the daughters of men were beautiful; and they took wives for themselves, whomever they chose.*

These sons of God or fallen angels mingled with the daughters of men breaking Gods commandment and produced a corruption of the flesh called: Nephilim, or Giants. Goliath and Og, king of Bashan, are examples of these giants in the bible.

Since we know the bible tells us that Noah was perfect in his lineage, the next question is who was Noah's wife? Was she of another race? The bible does not help us with this question nor does it give her name. But looking at the non-canonical book: The book of Jubilees, which is considered canonical by the Ethiopian Orthodox Church, and said to have been written 100 BC, we find both her name and who she is.

> Jubilees 4:33, *And in the 25th Jubilee, Noah took himself a wife, and her name was Emzara, the daughter of Rake'el, the daughter of his fathers brother.*

So with Noah's wife as reported by the book of Jubilees to be in the lineage of his father's brother, that would lead us to believe that his wife had common ancestry with Noah, who was recorded to have come from a perfect ancestral line. Taking the next ancestral step we now can claim since that Noah and his wife had common ancestry, they then would produce children that would be of their same race.

The next and last step to settle the question of where the worlds races came from after the Noahide flood if it was world wide is who were Noah's sons wives? Was it they who were from different races? As the bible is silent on Noah's wife Emzara, it is also silent on who these three women were. Jumping back to the book of Jubilees we are given these three womens names.

> Jubilees 7: 14, *And he (Ham) built for himself a city and called its name after the name of his wife,* **Ne'elatama'uk**.
>
> Jubilees 7: 15, *Japheth saw it and became envious of his brother and he too built for himself a city and he called its name after the name of his wife,* **Adataneses**.
>
> Jubilees, 7: 16, *And Shem dwelt with his father Noah and he built a city close to his father on the mountain and he too called its name after the name of his wife,* **Sedeqetelebab.**

Moving outwards to one of the original **Seven Dead Sea Scrolls** discovered in 1946 by Bedouin shepherds, we find answers.

> "*Noah declares he is a righteous man who was worried about darkness.* **He marries his sons and daughters to the children of his brother** *for all his offspring in accordance with the law of the eternal statute.*" (col. 6, line 8)

Noah married all his sons and daughters to the children of his brother thus ensuring his grandchildren would be in the same ancestral line as he and his wife were.

NOTE: The bible does not follow Noah's daughters before or after the flood. They could have been in a different land with their husbands when the flood came.

Moving outwards again to the non-canonical book of Jasher, which is mentioned in the bible 3 times, we receive further information on who Noah married his three sons to. Jasher Ch. 5: 35, *Then Noah took three daughters of Eliakim, son of Methuselah, for wives for his sons as the Lord had commanded Noah.* Methuselah is Noah's grandfather. Looking in the bible book of Luke, we find Methuselah listed in Noah's lineage. Luke 3: 36, *...son of Cainan, the son of Arphaxad, the son of Shem,* **the son of Noah, the son of Lamech, 37, the son of Methuselah**, *the son of Enoch...* So the book of Jasher also tells us Noah kept his sons wives in his ancestral bloodline.

And finally looking in the Aprocrypha, a compilation of 14 books that used to be in the original KJV bible we find in the book called: Tobias.

> Tobias 4: 12, *Beware of all whoredom my son, and chiefly take a wife of the seed of thy fathers, and take not a strange women to wife which is not of they fathers tribe for we are the children of the prophets,* **Noe, (Noah)** *Abraham, Issac, and Jacob: remember my son, that* **our fathers from the beginning they all married wives of their own kindred**, *and were blessed in their children, and their seed shall inherit the land.*

So taking all these non-canonical books into consideration we find that they are in agreement that Noah, a man claimed by the bible to be perfect in his ancestry, also chose a wife of common ancestry, and for his three sons he also chose wives from his own tribe i.e. a common related bloodline. Taking the next step can we assume that since Noah, his wife, his sons, and their wives, were all from a common racial ancestry, would they not produce children racially matched with themselves? Or are we going to do a theological pole vault over genetic history and just say they inherited those same type of genes Adam and Eve were claimed by some to have had and were just able to pop out children of multiple races because it helps the story explain itself when nothing else makes sense? As with the story of Adam and Eve, there are also no biblical references of Noah or his sons producing children of other races.

I suggest that this claim from the modern Christian that Adam and Eve, and Noah and his sons were producing multi-racial offspring is nothing more than made up stories used to promote a non-biblical narrative that has been passed down by our fathers and accepted as truth by the church that is in the current state of apostasy.

Putting this timeline together we see the Noah flood story as a believable local event when following the simple suggestion of using the second prime root definition of "land" for the Hebrew word "erets" instead of the first root definition of "earth".

1. Noah built an Ark for his family and the local animals at the commandment of God.
2. God brought a flood upon the land that destroyed the corrupt flesh (Nephilim/ giants) that dwelt in that land.
3. When the flood subsided Noah and his family were able to start over in the same land with the animals that were with them in the Ark.
4. Since the flood was local, other races not in the flooded land were alive back then as their ancestors are alive today.

Isn't it strange how choosing one definition of a word over the other can cause generations of Christians to believe in an unexplainable narrative of the Noahide flood that is neither supported by the scientific genealogy or by the bible itself?

CHAPTER FOUR

ARE GODS OLD TESTAMENT DIETARY LAWS STILL IN EFFECT?

God created the heavens, the earth, and everything in between. But in His infinite wisdom He created certain animals to clean up his creation called earth. It was this crew, the unclean crew the Israelites were told not to consume in Leviticus and Deuteronomy. It is important to understand the concept of clean and unclean animals which are referenced in the bible as far back as Genesis 7.

> Gen. 7: 2, *You shall take with you of every clean animal by sevens, a male and his female; and of the animals that are not clean two, a male and his female.*

Today many Christians don't even know there are dietary laws in the bible and most of the ones that do know choose not to follow them out of apathy or out of a misunderstanding of relevant bible scripture.

Looking at the books of Leviticus 11, and Deuteronomy 14, you will find a comprehensive list of do's and dont's in regards to epicurean pursuits within the animal kingdom. The edible (clean animals) are the ones that chew the cud and have the hoof divided in two. These animals include the cow, sheep, and deer. The unclean animals not fit for consumption include lions, wolves, bears, and pigs. The unclean animals are carnivores. While clean birds are for consumption, the unclean include the eagle, vulture, owl, seagull, hawk, and bat. Again, carnivores. You may eat whatever has fins and scales in the oceans, lakes, and rivers. This leaves out shell fish and catfish who are the garbage clean up crew of these same waters. Even some insects are listed as safe for human consumption and they are the winged insects which walk on all fours that have jointed legs, i.e. locusts, crickets, and the grasshopper.

After a quick review of these dietary laws you will find one of the worlds favorite dishes on the unclean list. The swine. Yes the pig is a walking garbage receptacle. These scavengers will eat anything from trash to dead animals to human waste to even their own young if the opportunity presents itself.

Article: Why you should avoid pork, Dr. Axe. 10/31/16

"The pig is a scavenger and not meant for human consumption. Pigs are rather dirty animals and are the waste eliminators on the farm. There are reasons why the meat of the pig becomes saturated with toxins. The digestive system of a pig digests rather quickly what it eats so many toxins remain in its fatty tissues and therefore made available for your consumption.

Another issue is the pig has few functional sweat glands giving it few tools to rid its body of toxins. Consuming pork means consuming those toxins. According to the "World Health Organization", processed meat like ham, bacon, and sausage, causes cancer. The "International Agency for Research on Cancer", also classifies processed meat as a carcinogen. Again, something that causes cancer. Pigs also carry a variety of parasites in their bodies and some of those parasites are difficult to kill even when cooking. If some of these issues I listed is not cause for your concern then you might consider the common conditions of how 97% of the pigs in the U.S. are raised for your consumption in today's pig farms. These animals get no fresh air or exercise as they are cooped up in warehouses and fed a steady diet of harmful drugs to keep them breathing and make them grow faster and fatter. These same drugs often cause the pig to become crippled under their own excessive and unnatural weight gain. It's estimated that 70% of factory raised pigs have pneumonia when they go to the slaughter house because of the extreme over crowded conditions at factory warehouses. Their living conditions are so bad that the only way to keep some of these pigs barely alive at times is to misuse and over use antibiotics."

The ocean counterparts to the pig are the bottom feeders called Lobsters, Crabs, and Shrimp. These creations by God play an important role in cleaning up Gods seas by consuming toxic garbage and the decaying dead. These bottom feeders are like little trash cans sweeping the ocean floors looking for debris and dead sea animals to consume. Every year millions of people are exposed to under cooked shellfish which poses a huge threat with active parasites, viruses, and bacteria. Ocean issues like mining, sewage, and fuel emissions, heavy metals, and mercury, end up in the water and will build up in these shellfish over time contributing to their toxicity. Almost all shellfish contain mercury which is especially harmful to young children and pregnant women.

God not only created this crew to clean up the trash in His oceans, but He also created another set of sea life to clean the water itself. Look no further than oysters, mussels, and scallops, affectionately called: Filter Feeders. These stationary water filters pump large amounts of water over their gills trapping small pieces of silt, bacteria, and plant debris for their dinner. Their job is to purify the water as they make their own meals out of decaying material including but not limited to, pathogenic viruses, heavy metals, and nerve toxins.

The counterpart to the saltwater shellfish are freshwater catfish, clams, mussels, crayfish, and even fresh water shrimp. These guys have the same career as their ocean partners only their work environment is in our lakes, rivers, and streams. So it should be understood the more waste we dump into our oceans, lakes, and rivers, the greater risk of getting sick from eating shellfish. Witnessing all these health reports and medical studies that are finally catching up with what God warned us about long ago in the bible, there seems to be a consensus developing today that confirms that some animal life is just not fit for human consumption.

So when was the last time you heard a preacher or priest warn you about the dangers of consuming pork and lobsters? Today in your modern churches the Christian believes that Gods dietary laws are no longer valid or applicable to the New Testament believing crowd. Some believe that God has purified the unclean animals and fired them from the jobs that they were originally created for even though a pig still eats garbage, shellfish still eat the ocean decaying dead, and the filter feeders still purify the water from viruses and toxins.

Some point to Mark 7, for their validation.

> KJV Mark 7: 18, *And he saith unto them, Are ye so without understanding also? Do ye not perceive, that whatsoever thing from without entereth into the man, it cannot defile him;* 19, *because it entereth not into his heart, but into the belly, and goeth out into the draught, purging all meats?*

It is here where some Christians thinks Jesus has just cleaned all the unclean meats for human consumption. So instead of cherry picking scripture that validates, let us consider the whole story that educates.

Mark 7, starts out with the Pharisees pointing out that Jesus's disciples did not wash their hands before they eat in verse 5.

> Mark 7: 5, *The Pharisees and the scribes asked Him, "Why do Your disciples not walk according to the tradition of the elders, but eat their bread with impure hands?*

Jesus then begins to explain what can or cannot defile a man.

A BRIDGE OVER THE SINS OF YOUR FATHERS • 51

> Mark 7: 14, *After He called the crowd to Him again, He began saying to them, "Listen to Me, all of you, and understand:* 15, *there is nothing outside the man which can defile him if it goes into him; but the things which proceed out of the man are what defile the man.*

Jesus is talking in a "parable" which is defined as a comparison of two things, often done through a story that has two meanings. The Christian stops at verse 19, for his validation claims of purified unclean animals but one step further into verse 20 the true meaning of Jesus's parable begins to take shape.

> Mark 7: 20, *And he said, That which cometh out of the man, that defileth the man.*
> 21, *For from within, out of the heart of men, proceed evil thoughts, adulteries, fornications, murders,*
> 22, *thefts, covetousness, wickedness, deceit, lasciviousness, an evil eye, blasphemy, pride, foolishness:* 23, *all these evil things come from within, and defile the man.*

Evil thoughts, fornication's, thefts, murders, adulteries, coveting, wickedness, deceit, lasciviousness, and an evil eye. Is anyone interested in a dish made from these sins? Slander sandwich anyone? Its a parable folks and at the end of this story Jesus informs us how those evil things defile a man and it doesn't include what he is having for dinner.

Next on the list for the defense of consuming pork is Acts 10. This story starts out with a commentary on Cornelius, a Roman Centurion, and then dovetails to Peter the Apostle climbing a roof to pray.

> Acts 10: 9, *On the next day, as they were on their way and approaching the city, Peter went up on the housetop about the sixth hour to pray.* 10, *But he became hungry and was desiring to eat; but while they were making preparations, he fell into a trance;* 11, *and he saw the sky opened up, and an object*

> *like a great sheet coming down, lowered by four corners to the ground, 12, and there were in it all* kinds of *four-footed animals and crawling creatures of the earth and birds of the air. 13, A voice came to him, "Get up, Peter, kill and eat!"* **14, But Peter said, "By no means, Lord, for I have never eaten anything unholy and unclean."** 15, *Again a voice* came *to him a second time, "What God has cleansed, no* longer *consider unholy." 16, This happened three times, and immediately the object was taken up into the sky.*

Here again the Christian will put on the brakes, close the book, and consider the matter of clean meat settled. But as the Christian of today claims to understand what the Lord is saying to Peter over a thousand years ago, Peter, who is a personal witness to the conversation with the Lord informs us he does not understand whats going on.

> Acts 10: 17, *Now while* **Peter was greatly perplexed in mind** *as to what the vision which he had seen might be....*

The reason why Peter is confused is shown back in verse 14.

> Acts 10: 14, *But Peter said, "By no means, Lord, for I have never eaten anything unholy and unclean.*

Looking a little deeper into the meaning of verse 14, what Peter is telling us without saying it is He still believes Gods dietary laws are still in force and that means to us that not one of his Apostle peers or Jesus Christ Himself did not inform him that the Old Testament dietary laws were no longer relevant.

With that we go forward and find our answer to what this vision of unclean animals really meant in verse 29.

> Acts 10: 29, *And he said to them, "You yourselves know how unlawful it is for a man who is a Jew* (ancient Israelite) *to*

associate with a foreigner or to visit him; ***and yet God has shown me that I should not call any man unholy or unclean.***

Acts 10: 45, *While Peter was still speaking these words, the Holy Spirit fell upon all those who were listening to the message.* 46, ***All the circumcised believers who came with Peter were amazed, because the gift of the Holy Spirit had been poured out on the Gentiles also.***

So this story is not about eating lions and tigers and bears. Peter informs us that he finally understood that this vision was about God now clearing the way for the Gentiles to receive the gift of the Holy Spirit. Before the Gentiles where unclean, but God Himself cleansed them and showed this to Peter through a vision of unclean animals. The next act on the agenda was baptism for the Gentiles.

Acts 10: 48, *"Surely no one can refuse the water for these to be baptized who have received the Holy Spirit just as we* did, *can he?"* 49, *And he ordered them to be baptized in the name of Jesus Christ.*

So the story in Acts 10 is complete:

1. Peter believes he is still under Gods dietary laws.
2. God gives Peter a revelation of unclean animals that confuses Peter.
3. At a later point in time Peter admits that the revelation he was given from God was not about dietary laws but about the gentiles being cleansed by God and were now able to receive the-holy spirit and the right to baptism for the first time.
4. This means Peter as an Israelite, was still under Gods dietary laws. It also means Jesus never rescinded these laws and the other apostles never declared them null and void, and Gods revelation to Peter in Acts 10, did not cancel them.

Moving on to 1 Corinthians 10, we have Paul telling the Corinthians they can eat anything in the local market, but as always a deeper look into scripture is needed for clarity.

> 1 Corr. 10; 25, *Eat anything that is sold in the meat market without asking questions for conscience' sake;* 26. *FOR THE EARTH IS THE LORD'S, AND ALL IT CONTAINS.* 27, *If one of the unbelievers invites you and you want to go, eat anything that is set before you without asking questions for conscience' sake.*
>
> 28, *But if anyone says to you, "This is meat sacrificed to idols," do not eat* it, *for the sake of the one who informed* you, *and for conscience' sake;* 29, *I mean not your own conscience, but the other* man's; *for why is my freedom judged by another's conscience?*

So here we are told in Corinthians all meats are good to eat accept what is sacrificed to idols. But what has Paul told us his mission was? Was he not the apostle to the Gentiles?

> Romans 11: 13, *But I am speaking to you who are Gentiles. Inasmuch then as I am an apostle of Gentiles...*

Questions:
1. Where is Paul? Corinth.
2. Who are the Corinthians? Gentiles
3. Who is Paul speaking to? Corinthians i.e. Gentiles

> KJV 1 Corr. 12: 2, *Ye know that ye were* **Gentiles**, *carried away unto these dumb idols, even as ye were led.*
>
> NASB 1 Corr. 12: 2, *You know that when you were* **pagans**, you were *led astray to the mute idols, however you were led.*

In Corinthians Paul is ministering to pagan gentiles **not currently bound by Israelite dietary laws.** So he knows its enough for him to try and change an ingrained pagan religious belief system without telling them they can no longer eat the food of their own diet.

Paul finds himself in the same situation in Colossae in the book of Colossians speaking to the gentile Christian community in the ancient city in modern Turkey.

> Col. 2:16, *Therefore no one is to act as your judge in regard to food or drink or in respect to a festival or a new moon or a Sabbath day*

What we must understand is its one thing if God Himself puts your people under a set of dietary laws, its another if a stranger walks into your city and trys to do the same thing isn't it? This is what "turn the other cheek means". It is NOT an order given to believers, but a lesson given by Jesus to his apostles. Christ knew his apostles/disciples were going to be shaking the very foundations of long held religious belief systems of His future gentile converts with His new gospel. He knew his apostles had to be long suffering and have a long rope of patience and tolerance. That is why Jesus said if they smite you, turn the other cheek.

> Matt. 5: 1, *When Jesus saw the crowds, He went up on the mountain; and after He sat down,* **His disciples came to Him 2, He opened His mouth and began to teach them**, *saying,*

> Matt. 5: 38, *"You have heard that it was said, 'AN EYE FOR AN EYE, AND A TOOTH FOR A TOOTH.' 39, But I say to you, do not resist an evil person; but whoever slaps you on your right cheek, turn the other to him also. 40, If anyone wants to sue you and take your shirt, let him have your coat also. 41, Whoever forces you to go one mile, go with him two, 42, Give to him who asks of you, and do not turn away from him who wants to borrow from you. 43, "You have heard that*

> *it was said, 'YOU SHALL LOVE YOUR NEIGHBOR and hate your enemy.' 44, But I say to you, love your enemies and pray for those who persecute you,*

As one can see. These lessons by Jesus were given to His apostles and NOT the Christian follower. These apostles were instructed how to bring the gospel to the pagan gentiles in a non confrontational gentle way. So to think todays Christians try to use these scriptures, 1 Corinthians and Colossians, to validate their reasons for believing Gods dietary laws have been voided is an example of zero research or faulty research on their part.

The last line of defense left for the defenders of pork and lobsters is found in 1 Timothy.

> 1 Tim. 4: 1, *But the Spirit explicitly says that in later times some will fall away from the faith, paying attention to deceitful spirits and doctrines of demons, 2, by means of the hypocrisy of liars seared in their own conscience as with a branding iron,* 3, men *who forbid marriage* and advocate *abstaining from foods which God has created to be gratefully shared in by those who believe and know the truth. 4, For everything created by God is good, and nothing is to be rejected if it is received with gratitude; 5, for it is sanctified by means of the word of God and prayer.*

Here Paul is telling Timothy that in latter times some shall depart from the faith and these deluded hypocrites will advocate abstaining from food or meats, and all meats are good for consumption.

> KJV 1 Tim. 4: 3 *Forbidding to marry, and commanding to* **abstain from meats**, *which God hath created to be received with thanksgiving of them which believe and know the truth.*

NASB 1 Tim. 4: 3, men *who forbid marriage* and advocate ***abstaining from foods*** *which God has created to be gratefully shared in by those who believe and know the truth.*

Here we have a controversy between the KJV and the NASB bibles. The KJV focuses on "meat" while the NASB says its "foods" that are the concern in 1 Timothy.

The NASB version changes the entire meaning of the verse relating to Gods dietary laws. The NASB is called the Scholars bible and is recognized for being the most accurate literal word for word translation.

Article: https://faithfoundedonfact.com/the-5-most-accurate-bible-translations/

This article rates the most accurate bibles for the most literal translation of the word.

1. NASB (New American Standard Bible)
2. ESV (English Standard Version)
3. NET (New English Translation)
4. KJV (King James Version)
5. NKJV (New King James Version)

I would urge following the scholars consensus of relying on the highest ranking version of the bible for our answers. Now looking at 1 Tim. 4, we can see that that conversation is not about changing Israel's dietary laws. Its about a falling away of the saints at some point in the future led by impostors promoting a doctrine of demons. But looking deeper into verse 4, we find this, *"For **everything** created by God is good, and nothing is to be rejected if it is received with gratitude"*. Here we find a very liberal use of the word "everything". If we follow the train of thought that "everything" created by God is good for consumption then what about poisonous plants? Hemlock? Are poisonous mushrooms good for food too?

If we just take this story in its whole we find a warning from Paul to Timothy about a future time when impostors will lead away the saints and follow a demonic doctrine which includes abstaining from foods. There is no Godly command of the reversal of dietary laws mentioned in 1 Timothy. Paul is not saying no one should ever follow Gods dietary laws again. He is explaining what these demonic impostors are going to do at some point in the future.

So if we go back to Acts 10, and use this story as a guide to understanding Gods dietary laws as they relate to today we learn that:

1. Jesus has long passed and Peter, the apostle, is still following Gods dietary laws.
2. God did not rescind His dietary laws in Acts 10.
3. Therefore these laws are still in effect.
4. If you are not following Gods dietary laws, the life you are supposed to have to accomplish Gods will could be in jeopardy or cut short by eating unhealthy animals not meant for consumption.

Another consideration for the discerning individual is if you as a Christian are consuming meats that are identified as unclean by God then can you make the claim your body is a clean vessel unto the Lord? The next question to ask yourself is can the holy spirit dwell properly or even safely within an unclean vessel?

> Lev. 5: 2, *if a person* **touches any unclean thing, whether a carcass of an unclean beast** *or the carcass of unclean cattle or a carcass of unclean swarming things, though it is hidden from him and he is unclean,* **then he will be guilty**.

Free dictionary: Carcass – The dead body of an animal especially one slaughtered for food.

Is it on the Christian's mind of what kind of body God's holy spirit wishes to dwell in?

2 Cor. 6: 16, *Or what agreement has the temple of God with idols?* ***For we are the temple of the living God;*** *just as God said,* *"**I WILL DWELL IN THEM** AND WALK AMONG THEM; AND I WILL BE THEIR GOD, AND THEY SHALL BE MY PEOPLE.* 17, *"Therefore, COME OUT FROM THEIR MIDST AND BE SEPARATE," says the Lord.* ***"AND DO NOT TOUCH WHAT IS UNCLEAN; And I will welcome you.*** 18, *"And I will be a father to you, And you shall be sons and daughters to Me," Says the Lord Almighty.*

If the Christian of today chooses to ignore Gods dietary laws he does it not because God voided them, but because he either does not care about his health or he is ignorant of why God established these dietary laws of the Old Testament.

CHAPTER FIVE

IS THE GAY LIFESTYLE UNACCEPTABLE TO GOD?

In todays America if you are not black, a woman, or gay, in many social circles you are viewed as less than worthy of true citizenship. But one glance into todays churches we find a new phenomenon developing. The inclusion of the homosexual lifestyle. So what can be said about homosexuality in the church that hasn't already been said? God, who should be the final word on all issues of concern has spoken and for the bible believing Christian you would think this matter would have been settled long ago. But lending our ears to today's clergy tells us it is not.

The LGBTQ community pencils in their numbers as 4 to 5% of the country's population but others not from this community will tell you its much lower. One of the prevailing issues with regards to this community is the inclusion, the acceptance, and even the promotion of homosexuality within the church walls of America. By now its common knowledge that the Catholic Church has had a long history of employing gay priests, but today in the Protestant Churches the acceptance of this lifestyle has not only gained a foothold, it has cleared the way for the homosexual pastor.

The questions before us are:
1. Is homosexuality an unacceptable sin to God?

2. Can a gay priest or pastor lead a church that would be blessed by God?
3. And ultimately, will a congregation that is fully aware of their pastors homosexuality find their name written in the Lambs book of life?

Knowing that homosexuality has been hotly debated in the church for decades, I am confident the clergy must be familiar with Gods firm view on this issue. But for their own personal reasons many of todays churches are either silent on the subject or nonchalantly sweep Gods law aside in pursuit of friendship with the worlds popular culture. As many of the wavering churches and their clergy seek some form of reconciliation with the lifestyle God identifies as sin, the Christian as an individual must decide for himself which side of the fence he is on.

In Genesis 19, we find God destroying Sodom and Gomorrah with fire and in verse 5, we find out why.

> Gen. 19: 4, *Before they lay down, the men of the city, the men of Sodom, surrounded the house, both young and old, all the people from every quarter*
>
> 5, and they called to Lot and said to him, "Where are the men who came to you tonight? Bring them out to us that we may have relations with them."

What kind of a sin does the bible tell us the act of homosexuality is?

> Leviticus 18: 22, '*You shall not lie with a male as one lies with a female;* **it is an abomination.**

Merriam-Webster dictionary: Abomination – Something regarded with disgust or hatred.

So can we say the bible is telling us God considers homosexuality not just a sin but an abomination? Can we say that God is not only disgusted with homosexuality but also hates this sin? What does the Old Testament have to say about this issue?

> Lev. 20: 13, '*If* there is *a man who lies with a male as those who lie with a woman, both of them have committed a detestable act; they shall surely be put to death. Their bloodguiltiness is upon them.*

> 1 Kings 14: 24, *There were also male cult prostitutes in the land. They did according to all the **abominations** of the nations which the LORD dispossessed before the sons of Israel.*

The Old Testament seems pretty clear where God stands on this sin. Is that sin looked upon the same way in the New Testament by our unchanging God?

> Romans 1: 26, *For this reason God gave them over to degrading passions; for their women exchanged the natural function for that which is unnatural, 27, and in the same way also the men abandoned the natural function of the woman and burned in their desire toward one another, men with men committing indecent acts and receiving in their own persons the due penalty of their error.*

> 1 Timothy 1: 9, *realizing the fact that law is not made for a righteous person, but for those who are lawless and rebellious, for the ungodly and sinners, for the unholy and profane, for those who kill their fathers or mothers, for murderers 10, and immoral men and homosexuals and kidnappers and liars and perjurers, and whatever else is contrary to sound teaching,*

> 1 Corinthians 6: 9, *Or do you not know that the unrighteous will not inherit the kingdom of God? Do not be deceived; nei-*

> *ther fornicators, nor idolaters, nor adulterers, nor effeminate,* **nor homosexuals**,
>
> 10, *nor thieves, nor the covetous, nor drunkards, nor revilers, nor swindlers, will inherit the kingdom of God.*

Can it not be said that according to the bible the homosexual is unrighteous and will not inherit the kingdom of God? Is it just not clear enough what God is saying about this sin of homosexuality? Do you see any wiggle room for compromise in Gods description of this abomination? Is not this lifestyle in direct conflict with Gods plan for his creation of man?

> Gen. 1: 27, *God created man in His own image, in the image of God He created him; male and female He created them* 28, *God blessed them; and God said to them,* "**Be fruitful and multiply, and fill the earth.**"
>
> Matthew 19: 4, *And He answered and said, "Have you not read that He who created them from the beginning MADE THEM MALE AND FEMALE, 5, and said, 'FOR THIS REASON A MAN SHALL LEAVE HIS FATHER AND MOTHER AND BE JOINED TO HIS WIFE, AND THE TWO SHALL BECOME ONE FLESH'?*

Since we are told that Gods plan for man and woman is to be joined in one flesh and then be fruitful and multiply and fill the earth with children, where does the homosexual fit in to Gods ultimate plan for mankind? There is nothing in scripture saying two men shall become one flesh. There is no way on earth that the homosexual lifestyle can fulfill Gods commandment of being fruitful and multiplying on the earth.

The firmness and clarity of Gods decision on homosexuality in both the Old Testament and the New Testament leaves the discerning individual thinking on what grounds or theology is the church of today basing their acceptance and inclusion of homosexuality? Do these clergy feel they have the right or the ability to influence the will of the unchanging God?

> Isaiah 40: 8, *The grass withers, the flower fades, But the word of our God stands forever.*
>
> Malachi 3: 6, *For I, the LORD, do not change;...*
>
> Psalms 33: 11, *The counsel of the LORD stands forever, The plans of His heart from generation to generation.*
>
> Hebrews 13: 8, Je*sus Christ* is *the same yesterday and today and forever.*

As I began researching which churches accepted the gay lifestyle and gay clergy the list was incredible. From Anglicans to Catholics, Presbyterians to Pentecostals, Methodists to Lutherans, and even Baptists. It is clear that these mainstream denominations have pushed aside Gods laws for friendship with the world. Since there was a time in the Churches history when homosexuality was preached to the world as a sin we need to look at when and what changed the churches position on this volatile subject.

Article: Metrosource.com 6/12/2019 – This is why more Christians now support LGBTQ relationships.

> "More and more Christians realize it is a grievous sin to treat LGBTQ people as many churches have in the past. Its important to realize that Christians are moving beyond tolerance into real acceptance."

So basically this article is saying its a sin not to accept a sinful lifestyle.

Article: Blogs.bible.org 6/30/2015 – Why have so many Christians and Churches become pro-gay?

"There are two reasons why,

1. Rejecting the authority of Gods word. The bitter fruit of several decades of shallow preaching and discipleship and ignoring or flat out rejecting unmistakably clear biblical statements condemning homosexual relationships.
2. The surrender to the gay agenda. The gay manifesto was spelled out in a book called: After the Ball: How America will conquer its fear and hatred of Gays in the 90's. Written by Marshall Kirk and Hunter Madsen.

This 6 point manifesto marketing plan spelled out in Marshalls and Hunters book is as follows:

1. Desensitization and normalization of homosexuals in mainstream America.
2. Portray members of the LGBTQ community as victims.
3. Give protectors a just cause – anti-discrimination.
4. The use of TV, Music, Film, and Social Media, to desensitize mainstream Americans.
5. Portray Gays and Lesbians as pillars of society.
6. Once homosexuals have begun to gain acceptance, anti-gay opponents must be vilified."

This 6 point marketing plan was executed perfectly with the assistance of Hollywood, the music industry, the U.S. Government, and this nations schools. So I guess I can say with much confidence that it was a couple of gay guys marketing plan that literally changed the Churches stance on homosexuality which ended up causing the Church to reject Gods law regarding this abomination. Can it be said that when confronted with the decision between following Gods laws or mans marketing plan the Church chose the latter?

Article: Baptistnews.com 2/13/2018 – 10 things we're learning about the LGBTQ debate in Church.

> "Our congregation went through 18 months of intense study and prayer and dialogue about the LGBTQ inclusions and we

have the scars regardless of which way the decision went. But we are better for choosing the good over the easy. Our decision to become fully inclusive of LGBTQ caused us to lose 270 members but that same decision gave us 135 new members who wanted to be part of an inclusive congregation. A good outcome for them and us."

Basically this Baptist Church chased out 270 bible believing God fearing Christians so they could accommodate the lifestyle of sinners. I am positive God Himself will remember what this Churches idea of "what a good outcome is".

Then there is the claim by those who defend the morality of homosexuality that gay people were born that way therefore same sex relationships are normal for them. So that means we are to believe mans genetic claim over Gods genetic claim. Are we to believe the sinner when he tells us God made a mistake? Even secular science is having trouble with this one.

Article: arcapologetics.org 3/19//2014 – Abandoning Nature: Some reasons why homosexuality is wrong.

"Scientific research based on the work of Michael Baily and Richard Pillar assert "our own research has shown that male sexual orientation is substantially genetic." (A genetic study of male sexual orientation archives of General Psychiatry. 48 1991 1089-66)"

As you should know I could list more studies exemplifying the same result given here but for every article validating this study there will be someone out there who is pushing the gay agenda trying to invalidate it.

What the Church can do is promote healing as this type of sexual activity has been medically proven that it can be cured by motivated patients, while also taking a strong stand against inclusion of this sinful lifestyle.

So would it take just one more verse of scripture than what is already there in the bible to convince the Christian that God calls homosexuality an abomination? This argument, if one can actually sign on to the thinking that this is an actual argument, was settled by God long before Marshall Kirk and Hunter Madsen wrote their manifesto marketing plan for the acceptance of homosexuality. Today the Church has a choice in this issue. Follow Gods laws and plan for salvation or follow Marshall and Hunters marketing plan for the acceptance of homosexuality. Gods definition of this sin outlined in the bible proves to the discerning Christian that there is no middle ground.

> Romans 12: 1, *Therefore I urge you, brethren, by the mercies of God, to present your bodies a living and holy sacrifice, acceptable to God,* which is *your spiritual service of* worship. 2, And *do not be conformed to this world, but be transformed by the renewing of your mind, so that you may prove what the will of God is, that which is good and acceptable and perfect.*

CHAPTER SIX

THE BIBLICAL ROLE FOR WOMEN DEFINED IN GODS NATURAL ORDER

As with the homosexual issue, this issue about the role of women in the Christian family has been hotly contested and hotly debated. Todays woman is heavily influenced by Hollywood and pop culture as many of the female persuasion no longer have the biblical desire to assume her place in Gods natural order as her husbands help meet. From the silver screen to the TV screen is where the woman sees her female heros portrayed as man beating, foul mouthed, promiscuous floozies. And of course the man is often portrayed as the weaker and dumber sex. In todays world if women and girls are not grounded in reality they can actually begin to believe these faerie tale stories of a 5 foot, 3 inch, 105 pound girl dropping a 6 foot, 200 pound man with one punch. Just how far can this culture of female gender promotion bordering on worship go?

Historically speaking, once the woman secured the right to vote the next stop was out of the house and into the work place. Once there she needed special laws written to protect her from all those men that were already there. With gender based scholarships and special privileges in the work place, she was armored up for her new found war against the pop culturally described historically oppressive male.

But an odd thing happened along the way in the woman's pursuit to free herself from Gods natural order. With the shackles of motherhood sufficiently demoted to a negative cultural status....

Enter the transgender woman.

For those of us who were there, we were all ringside witnesses of how America's elevation of the woman was forced upon the culture through laws and special privileges in the 60's and 70's so they could be in direct competition with man, But today Americas pop culture and the U.S. Government has now welcomed the transgender woman to be in direct competition with the real woman.

Where once the stay at home moms and grandmothers would donate their time to read to the children at the local library, now we have "drag queen story hour" to replace them both. This new story hour is lead by a man dressed up as some bizarre looking type of female that not only reads to your children but also promotes his ideology to their young impressionable minds. To the drag queens its not just about story reading.

From their website: dragqueenstoryhour.org,

> "Drag Queen story hour is a fun and important program that celebrates diversity in the way that children "may dress and act." It encourages children to look beyond gender stereotypes and embrace unfettered exploration of self."

Having successfully planted chapters in 27 states including international chapters these shemales have now set their sights on womens sports.

Article: As reported by the EU Times on 2/22/21.

One of (fake) president Joe Biden's first acts in office was to sign an executive order on preventing and combating discrimination on the basis of gender identity or sexual orientation. This order declares that (gender switching) children should be able to learn without worrying about whether they will be denied access to restrooms, locker rooms, or school sports. This woke policy officially endorses biological males competing against biological females in womens sports, and since then these "shemales" have been making quite a name for themselves in this endeavor.

- Franklin Pierce University senior male Cece Telfer became an NCAA womans track and field champion in 2019.
- Male – Mary Gregory in the spring of 2019, dominated at the Raw Power lifting federation competition in Virginia.
- Males – Terry Miller and Andraya Yearwood dominated a Connecticut High School womens track championship in 2019.
- Male – Rachel McKinnon set the world record for womens sprint world championship in 2019.
- As reported by the Western Journal on 4/3/2022, Fallon Fox, a transgender MMA fighter who broke a womans skull in the ring has now been called the bravest athlete in history.

The next target for the transgender dudes was the womans fashion industry. Not fulfilled with knocking women out of the ring they now are pushing them off the fashion runways.

Article: These 22 Trans Models Are Revolutionizing the Fashion Industry June 3, 2022 https://www.popsugar.com/fashion/Transgender-Models-41954393

In recent years, the fashion industry has made more progress toward inclusive representation of transgender models.

Some newer brands like New York City-based label Chromat have included trans models in runway shows and advertising campaigns early on, while other household names have made these changes much later, most notably with Victoria's Secret hiring its first transgender model, Valentina Sampaio in August 2019 and later hiring its first Black transgender model, Emira D'Spain, in February 2022.

Then there is Chanel recruiting 25-year-old Teddy Quinlivan as a new beauty face the same year.

Teddy Quinlivan

Just how far does America want to push this transgender issue?

Enter Dr. Rachel Levine, (Fake) President Joe Bidens Assistant Health Secretary, named in March 2022 by USA Today, Woman of the Year. A senior Biden health appointee who made history when he/she became the nation's highest-ranking openly transgender official, has also become its first openly transgender four-star officer across any of the country's eight uniformed services.

Here he is, lipstick and all. I guess in todays America it takes a real man to be a woman.

Do you consider it peculiar or poetic justice as women reject their role in Gods ordained natural order, today they are being replaced by an aberration of themselves?

So as these women wannabe's push the real women aside in our libraries, our sports, the fashion industry, this nations awards, and bathrooms, do you catch yourself wondering where are all the feminist heros in this debate?

- Article: Elephant Journal 9/12/2017 – Why my feminism includes transgender women.
- Article: Buzzfeed News 12/22/2018 – Feminist Academics explain why they support transgender rights.
- Tedtalk: Amelia Abraham 2019 – Talk Title: Why Feminists should support transgender rights.
- Article: Huff Post 2/12/2016 – Feminist issues are transgender issues.
- Article: Bazaar 7/10/20 – When Feminism supports trans rights everyone benefits.

Isn't that just interesting? The crew that screamed the loudest and longest for womens rights are now fighting for the mens right to replace them. Is it time to start questioning other possible motives these feminists might have been harboring all these years? To explore that question we are going to have to step sideways and out of our comfort zone to review a little known interview of one Aaron Russo in 2007 and of his attempted recruitment to the NWO by Nicholas Rockefeller,

> Aaron Russo, February 14, 1943 – August 24, 2007, was an American businessman, film producer, director, and political activist. Recognized by the Rockefellers as a mover-shaker they attempted, but failed to recruit him for their New World Order Club. In a 12 minute video with Alex Jones, Russo discussed one of his conversations with Nicholas Rockefeller. He was told by Nicholas Rockefeller 11 months before 911 that an event was going to happen that will begin the (phony) war on terrorism. In the 9th minute of this video Russo begins telling us that Nicholas told him that it was the Rockefellers who were the ones that funded the womens liberation movement. Russo's first response was "this is a positive thing to give women the vote and equal pay in the workforce" but he was immediately corrected by Nicholas who informed him that the real agenda behind the womens lib movement was to

get the kids into school at an earlier age to indoctrinate them and break up the nuclear family. Another reason was doubling the tax base with both parents in the work force.

To listen to this interview on youtube:
Aaron Russo talks to the Rockefeller Elite
https://www.youtube.com/watch?v=7gwcQjDhZtI

Russo rejected Rockefellers invitation to join the NWO because he said he had no interest in enslaving people.

Marching to Rockefellers orders, the womens liberation movement lost touch with, rejected, and sometimes literally ran over the woman who was in Gods natural order, as the roles of wife and mother were the casualties of this organizations war on men. These same women eagerly embraced Rockefellers vision of two parents in the workforce therefore causing their children to be raised in Day Care facilities and then marshaled off to school at an earlier age in pre-school to begin their indoctrination.

There is the old saying, "you reap what you sow." So what has the womans war on Gods natural order brought to themselves, their families, and the world?

1. Article: Brookings.edu 9/1/1996 – Since 1970 out of wedlock birthrates have soared.
2. Article: r4dn.com 7/6/2020 – Why has the divorce rate increased since the 1970's?
3. AskingLot.com 7/1/2020 – How much has the prison population increased since the 1970's?

Enough time has passed and enough statistical evidence has been documented to successfully assist the thinking person to understand that Gods natural order for the family and Rockefellers womens liberation movement create two distinct outcomes. If todays increase in single parent families, increased divorce rates, and soaring crime rates, impress you, then your desired family goals matches Rockefellers womens liberation movement goals.

Gods plan for mankind is clear and concise and leaves nothing for the confused Christian to debate about. In Genesis 2, we are told that Adam was formed into a man with a soul. Then God made His decision to give Adam a wife.

> Gen. 2: 18, *Then the LORD God said, "It is not good for the man to be alone; I will make him a **helper** suitable for him."*

You will notice God is using the term "helper" to describe the role of his soon to be female companion.

Free Dictionary.com: Helper – to give assistance (to someone) make it easier for (someone) to do something.

A helper is not described as a leader or a decision making equal. Clearly God wanted Adam to have his female companion give him assistance in his life endeavors. After Eve brought on the fall of man, God re-defined her role and with it the role of future women.

> Gen. 3: 16, *To the woman He said, "I will greatly multiply Your pain in childbirth, In pain you will bring forth children; Yet your desire will be for your husband, And he will rule over you."*

The modern Christian woman who is having problems with Gods decision in Gen. 3:16, is of the mind that God either made a mistake or He didn't get the Rockefeller memo claiming that women no longer need to be wives and mothers to reach true womanhood. There are even many Christian men today who have a problem with God placing the woman in a submissive role under their leadership. These same men who like to call their wife "the boss lady" should be questioning their own fitness for leadership in Gods natural order for the family.

For those Christian women who claim that they are under New Testament grace and no longer bound to Gods Old Testament ordained natural order, a little research will either help you or depress you.

1 Corr. 11: 3, *But I want you to understand that Christ is the head of every man, and the man is the head of a woman, and God is the head of Christ.*

1 Corr. 11: 7, *For a man ought not to have his head covered, since he is the image and glory of God; but the woman is the glory of* man. 8, For *man does not originate from woman, but woman from man;* 9, *for indeed man was not created for the woman's sake, but woman for the man's sake.*

Eph. 5: 22, *Wives,* be subject *to your own husbands, as to the Lord.* 23, *For the husband is the head of the wife, as Christ also is the head of the church, He Himself* being *the Savior of the body.* 24, *But as the church is subject to Christ, so also the wives* ought to be *to their husbands in everything.*

Col. 3: 18, *Wives, be subject to your husbands, as is fitting in the Lord.*

Titus 2: 5, (women) to be *sensible, pure, workers at home, kind, being subject to their own husbands, so that the word of God will not be dishonored.*

From the creation of Eve in the Old Testament through the New Testament the biblical theme is consistent, clear, and unwavering for those who have ears to hear. God has designed a Natural Order for mankind. 1. God the Father, 2. Jesus the Son, 3. Man, 4. Woman. 1 Corr. 11: 3.

Yet still some women climb over a mountain of scripture to pastor churches today pretending the bible is silent on this issue.

1 Tim. 2: 12, *But I do not allow a woman to teach or exercise authority over a man, but to remain quiet.*

1 Corr. 14: 34, *The women are to keep silent in the churches; for they are not permitted to speak, but are to subject themselves, just as the Law also says.* 35, *If they desire to learn*

> *anything, let them ask their own husbands at home; for it is improper for a woman to speak in church.*

So who does the bible say is approved to oversee and pastor a church:

> 1 Tim. 3: 1, *It is a trustworthy statement: if any **man** aspires to the office of overseer, it is a fine work he desires to do. 2, An overseer, then, must be above reproach, the **husband of one wife**, temperate, prudent, respectable, hospitable, able to teach, 3, not addicted to wine or pugnacious, but gentle, peaceable, free from the love of money. 4, **He must be** one who manages his own household well, **keeping his children under control with all dignity.***

Am I the only one who cannot find one reference to a woman being described as a proper fit for the office of pastor in the bible? So where is the biblical authority that allows these women to pastor churches? Since Paul is telling us in 1 Corr. 14, that it is <u>Gods law</u> that a woman cannot speak in churches, are these woman pastors claiming they are above the Gods law? Is the congregation that attends a church pastored by a woman claiming also to above Gods Law? The biblical argument today for recognizing the authority of women pastors ranges from wishful thinking to taking an embarrassing amount of liberty with bible scripture to justify such thinking.

Argument 1: Yes women can teach in the ministry but they must avoid using the masculine noun "pastor" when outlining their role.

Response: I think I will just let this claim of switching titles to validate women pastors speak for itself.

Argument 2: 1 Tim. 2: 12, Shouldn't be taken literally because women then could not become doctors, professors, or high school teachers, because this verse does not say it is restricted to the church.

A BRIDGE OVER THE SINS OF YOUR FATHERS • 79

Response: If we take another look at 1 Timothy, as a whole including the other related chapters, a continual theme throughout this book answers this stated question of verse 12.

Chapter 1:

1 Tim. 1: 3, *As I urged you upon my departure for Macedonia, remain on at Ephesus so that you may* **instruct** *certain men not to* **teach** *strange* **doctrines.**

1 Tim. 1: 5, *But the* **goal of our instruction** *is love from a pure heart and a good conscience and a sincere faith.*

1 Tim. 1: 8, *But we know that* **the Law** *is good, if one uses it lawfully*

1 Tim 1: 11, *according to the* **glorious gospel** *of the blessed God, with which I have been entrusted.*

In chapter 1, Paul is talking about the **goals of teaching doctrines** based on the **law of the gospel.** In chapter 2, Paul begins to itemize the issues of what is to be taught in the church.

Chapter 2:

1 Tim. 2: 1, F*irst of all, then, I urge that entreaties* and *prayers, petitions* and *thanksgivings, be made on behalf of all men.*

1 Tim. 2: 9, *Likewise,* I want *women to adorn themselves with proper clothing, modestly and discreetly, not with braided hair and gold or pearls or costly garments,*

1 Tim. 2: 12, *But I do not allow a woman to teach or exercise authority over a man, but to remain quiet.*

By the 3rd chapter, Paul informs Timothy (and the reader) "why" he is writing these things to him outlined in the first two chapters.

Chapter 3:

1 Tim. 3: 14, *I am writing these things to you, hoping to come to you before long;* 15, *but in case I am delayed,* ***I write so that you will know how one ought to conduct himself in the household of God****, which is the church of the living God, the pillar and support of the truth.*

So instead of focusing on just verse 12 to assume validation for the authority of the female pastor, shouldn't we be looking at the whole story?

Paul is clearly instructing Timothy in these 3 chapters how one should conduct themselves IN CHURCH. Not one mention of future doctor professions for women, female professor jobs, or female high school teachers is there?

Argument 3: Women can preach but they cannot teach. (Yes you actually read that) This is actually a real argument outlined in a book on this subject called: Hearing Her Voice; A biblical invitation for women to preach, by John Dickson. Dickson claims there are several ways to speak in church as in exhorting, prophesying, and preaching, which as he sees it, does not apply to the term – teaching.

Response: If the bible is our final authority on "was Gods law taught?" Then when an argument relies heavily on first century text you will expect the earliest centuries of the church to re-enforce your argument and not undermine it.

Old Testament

Deut. 4: 1, *Now, O Israel, listen to the* ***statutes and the judgments*** *which* ***I am teaching you*** *to perform, so that you may live and go in and take possession of the land which the LORD, the God of your fathers, is giving you.*

2 Chron. 15: 3, *For many days Israel was without the true God and without a* ***teaching priest*** *and without law.*

2 Chron. 17: 9, **They taught** in Judah, having the **book of the law** of the LORD with them; and they went throughout all the cities of Judah **and taught** among the people.

Ezra 7: 10, *For Ezra had set his heart to study the law of the LORD and to practice it, and to **teach** His **statutes and ordinances** in Israel.*

New Testament

Matt. 7: 28, *When Jesus had finished these words, the crowds were amazed at His **teaching**; 29, for He was teaching them as one having authority, and not as their scribes*

Luke 3: 12, *And some tax collectors also came to be baptized, and they said to him, "**Teacher,** what shall we do?*

Acts 5: 42, *And every day, in the temple and from house to house, they kept right on **teaching** and preaching Jesus as the Christ.*

1 Tim. 2: 7, *For this I was appointed a preacher and an apostle (I am telling the truth, I am not lying)* **as a teacher** *of the Gentiles in faith and truth.*

Citing the authority of the Old Testament, two gospels, and the New Testament, with much confidence we can understand that the Lords Law was passed on by the institution of – Teaching.

1. There are texts
2. There are teachers
3. There is a congregation

So Mr. Dicksons argument for women that preaching, exhorting, and prophesying, will confirm their authority to preach, is not biblically supported. Moses, the Prophets, the Apostles, and Christ, were all teachers of Gods gospel and teaching was the way the people received that same gospel. But here again, Paul tells Timothy women are supposed to silent in church. So how would Mr. Dickson exhort around that?

Some point to the story of Priscilla and Aguila and say they were acting as teaching pastors in the bible book of Acts.

> Acts 18: 24, *Now a Jew named Apollos, an Alexandrian by birth, an eloquent man, came to Ephesus; and he was mighty in the Scriptures.* 25, *This man had been instructed in the way of the Lord; and being fervent in spirit, he was speaking and teaching accurately the things concerning Jesus, being acquainted only with the baptism of John* 26, *and he began to speak out boldly in the synagogue.* **But when Priscilla and Aquila heard him, they took him aside and explained to him the way of God more accurately.**

How does standing behind a podium of a church and preaching to a congregation even remotely resemble taking someone aside in a synagogue and explaining some issues to them? Priscilla and Aguila made another appearance in Romans 16, but are still not preaching in front of a congregation.

> Romans 16: 3, *Greet Prisca (Priscilla) and Aquila, my fellow workers in Christ Jesus,*

This husband and wife were not introduced as apostles, pastors, deacons, or clergy of any kind, but as workers.

Lastly we can look at the example of Deborah, the Prophetess.

> Judges 4: 4, *Now Deborah, a prophetess, the wife of Lappidoth, was judging Israel at that time.* 5, *She used to sit under the palm tree between Ramah and Bethel in the hill country of Ephraim; and the sons of Israel came up to her for judgment.*

Here again the bible is clear. She is a Prophetess, not a preacher or a teacher. She is not leading a congregation in a church. Judges 4, tells us she sits under a palm tree and is visited by the sons of Israel. What this bible story tells us is a woman can be a prophet of God.

The bible has spoken on this subject in a clear and a concise language. Women are not to pastor churches. Women can be prophets and they can work in a church. They can talk to women's groups in church. I would imagine they can teach a Sunday school class to young children of both boys and girls because that activity does not violate Gods commandment of women being silent in the congregational service and they would not be teaching men. God has spoken and delivered to His people His natural order for mankind. If the woman rejects Gods order for the Christian family then she is rejecting Gods plan for His people. If you choose not to be in His plan then can you claim to be counted among His people?

It has been said....."you cannot break Gods laws, you can only break yourself against them"

Many women today struggle with the biblical concept of submission in marriage because they mistakenly equate being submissive with being inferior. In Gods eyes both males and females are blessed in different ways. The bible says nothing about the woman being inferior or about the man being superior. God is clear about His role for men as husbands.

> Eph. 5: 25, *Husbands, love your wives, just as Christ also loved the church and gave Himself up for her.* **LOVE**

> 1 Peter 3: 7, *You husbands in the same way, live with your wives in an understanding way, as with someone weaker, since she is a woman; and show her honor as a fellow heir of the grace of life, so that your prayers will not be hindered.*
> **HONOR**

> Col. 3: 19, *Husbands, love your wives and do not be embittered against them* **DO NOT BE ANGRY WITH HER**

> Gen. 2: 24. *For this reason a man shall leave his father and his mother, and be joined to his wife; and they shall become one flesh.* **MAN SHALL LEAVE HIS PARENT AND BE JOINED TO THE WIFE**

So how can a wife be biblically inferior to her husband when God has commanded man to love his wife, honor her, do not be angry with her, and have her to be placed above his own parents? The husband does not assume the role of boss in the marriage. He is tasked with leadership, protector, spiritual guidance, and putting the needs of the wife and family first above his own. If the Christian man is not living up to his God given duties as a husband and father then a spiritual assessment of his character as a Christian must be conducted by himself and/or a reliable Christian counselor or a trusted friend or relation.

Gods natural order for the christian marriage and family is designed to promote unity, harmony, and order, as the husband and wife take their journey in life. The woman who cannot accept her place in the God ordained Christian marriage will create competition and contention in her relationship with her husband. The woman who values contemporary social culture over Gods biblical teachings will never find true happiness outside of Gods natural order for the marriage.

> 1 Corr. 11: 2, *But I want you to understand that Christ is the head of every man, and the man is the head of a woman, and God is the head of Christ.*

CHAPTER SEVEN

THE TRINITY THAT NEVER WAS

Todays Christians seem to mostly agree that God, Jesus, and the Holy Ghost are one in the same, kind of. This concept is not very easily explained. I myself have asked the Christian to walk me through this process and even they get a little confused as they try to tell me what the Trinity is.

The "christianwakeupcall.com" explains it like this:

> "The Trinity simply put, refers to God being one person, but existing in three coexisting , co-eternal, co-substantial persons. God the Father, God the Son, and God the Holy Spirit. They are distinctive and connect with us meaningfully in different ways, but they are one. We worship all three as equals when we worship God."

So a person who did not grow up with this Trinity concept is asked to believe that God the Father birthed Himself and became His own Son. All the while still claiming to be the Father of Himself. But add to that mix that the Holy Ghost as a separate entity also resides in God and even outside God at the same time. To further add to the confusion Jesus tells us this:

> Luke 22: 69, *But from now on THE SON OF MAN WILL BE SEATED AT THE RIGHT HAND of the power OF GOD.*

Not at Gods left hand, not behind Him, but at the right hand of the power of God. To promote this Trinity thinking why did not Jesus say He would be sitting on the right hand of Himself? And then there is this:

> Matt. 3: 16, *After being baptized, Jesus came up immediately from the water; and behold, the heavens were opened, and he saw the Spirit of God descending as a dove* and *lighting on Him,* 17, *and behold, a voice out of the heavens said, "This is My beloved Son, in whom I am well-pleased."*

So here we are told to believe God the Father is pleased with Himself, as a Son, and that His Son, really Himself, got baptized. Which I guess could mean they both got baptized? Moving on to John we get this.

> John 17: 1, *Jesus spoke these things; and lifting up His eyes to heaven, He said, "Father, the hour has come; glorify Your Son, that the Son may glorify You,* 2, *even as You gave Him authority over all flesh, that to all whom You have given Him, He may give eternal life.*

Here I guess Jesus is praying to Himself as He says God the Father, or He Himself, gave Himself the Son authority over all flesh. It must be understood I am not mocking God, Jesus, or the Holy Ghost, but framing this concept with the scripture the trinity believers want me to believe. But looking at Matthew 24, this Trinity concept is pushed to a new level.

> Matt. 24: 36, *"But of that day and hour no one knows, not even the angels of heaven, nor the Son, but the Father alone.*

Here Jesus says He doesn't know the hour, but only the Father, who is really Himself knows. So Jesus really does know, but is claiming only He as the Father Knows as He as the Son does not. I truly mean no disrespect but just standing back looking at the Trinity in some sort of rational way it appears very irrational.

The word "Trinity" does not exist in the bible but there are three scriptures that give us a sense of God the Father, Jesus the Son, and the Holy Ghost, are actually <u>working together as one</u>.

1. NASB John 10: 30, *I and the Father are one."*

2. NASB Isaiah 9: 6, *For a child will be born to us, a son will be given to us; And the government will rest on His shoulders; And His name will be called Wonderful Counselor, Mighty God, Eternal Father, Prince of Peace.*

3. **KJV** 1 John 5: 7, *"For there are three that bear witness in heaven: The Father, the Word, and the Holy Spirit; and these three are one.*

Considering the first above listed scripture, John 10. It only claims the Father and Jesus are one and left out mentioning the Holy Ghost. So really there can be no trinity without the Holy Ghost. Could this be another one of Jesus's metaphors so often used in the bible?

Considering the second listed scripture, Isaiah 9. Isaiah gives Jesus the title: prince of peace, but at the same time calls Him the eternal father, and also Wonderful Counselor, and then Mighty God. It sounds like Isaiah is just describing Jesus in many worshiping words. But again, no Holy Ghost mentioned so here we have another incomplete description of a Trinity.

Finally considering 1 John 5: 7, we have a problem. You will notice I used the **KJV** to list 1 John 5: 7. But when we compare the NASB bible version of verse 7 with the KJV version we get a whole different story.

> **KJV** 1 John 5: 7, *"For there are three that bear witness in heaven: The Father, the Word, and the Holy Spirit; and these three are one.*
>
> **NASB** 1 John 5: 7, *For there are three that testify:*

That's all verse 7 says in the NASB. This means we have a translation issue between the NASB and the KJV. The KJV seems to have a lot more descriptive words promoting the idea of a Trinity in verse 7, than the NASB does in this same verse. Taking the next step to verse 8, both versions seem to get back into some form of alignment.

> **NASB** 1 John 5: 8, *the Spirit and the water and the blood; and the three are in agreement.*
>
> **KJV** 1 John 5: 8, *And there are three that bear witness in earth, the spirit, and the water, and the blood: and these three agree in one.*

So what we have is the KJV and the NASB are in total disagreement with each other in verse 7. Here is where the reader has to make a judgment call as to which version they will choose to believe.

The NASB was written in 1970, and is called the Scholars Bible because it is said to be the best literal word for word translation. The KJV is said to have been written in 1611. The NASB has earned the reputation of being the most accurate English Bible translation. The *New American Standard Bible* update (1995) carried on the NASB tradition of being a true Bible translation revealing what the original manuscripts actually say—not merely what the translator believes they mean.

So we are left with two different stories and two different translations. One bible (KJV) has been in the hands of the Catholic Church for a very long time and it was that church that not only invented the concept of the Trinity but demanded belief in it through enforced compliance. The other bible (NASB) was not under the influence of the Catholic Church when it was written. Choose your path Christian.

In defense of the Trinity doctrine this article will be cited. I will put my commentary after each of the following 6 numbered points in this article.

Article: zondervanacademic.com 12/15/17–Is the Trinity in the bible?

1. "A (trinity) doctrine so defined can be spoken of as a biblical doctrine only on the principle that the sense of scripture is scriptures and the definition of a biblical doctrine in such unbiblical language can be justified only on the principle that it is better to preserve the truth of scripture than the words of scripture."

My Commentary: What I can glean from this statement is the Trinity doctrine can only be defined on the principle that it is better to preserve the truth of scripture even though it is in unbiblical language, than to believe the actual words of scripture.

2. "Put simply, if forced to choose, the theologian would have to choose the truth of scripture, rather than the words of scripture."

My Commentary: A theologian must choose the truth of scripture as he or someone would personally define it, rather than choose to believe the real words of scripture.

3. "When speaking of the Trinity, theological usage must make the leap from direct biblical language to its own helpful vocabulary."

My Commentary: When talking about the Trinity, one must not use direct biblical language but use ones own made up vocabulary.

4. "Trinity theology cultivates both the sound of scriptures own language and the sense of those words, given new articulation by new interpreters."

My Commentary: The Trinity theology sounds like bible scriptures but it has its own language and needs interpreters to articulate it in a new way.

5. "Christians have always claimed they got the doctrine of Trinity from the bible itself. While acknowledging they had rendered the doctrine more explicit, and also admitting they had manufactured a set of extra biblical terms to help them articulate it with greater clarity."

My Commentary: Trinity believing Christians admit they had to manufacture a new set of non-biblical terms to help them articulate their Trinity doctrine.

This article ends with this comment from its author:

6. "But in our own time it has become crucial for Trinitarian theology to demonstrate as directly as possible that it is biblical."

My Commentary: All 6 points discussed in this article admit in unique and consistent ways that the bible does not describe the existence of the doctrine of Trinity, and that the Christian had to manufacture a set of new un-biblical terms to justify belief in this doctrine so that they could choose the truth of what they believe the scripture should say as opposed to what the words of the bible actually is saying.

Doesn't sound like this pro-Trinity advocate is really sure about anything is he?

So where did this Trinity doctrine come from and who brought it into existence? We will cite this article:

https://www.ucg.org/bible-study-tools/booklets/is-god-a-trinity/the-surprising-origins-of-the-trinity-doctrine

Article: Beyond Today: The Surprising origins of the Trinity Doctrine. 6/22/2011.

"Barely two decades after Christs death and resurrection the apostle Paul wrote that many believers were already turning away to a different gospel.

> Gal. 1: 6, *I am amazed that you are so quickly deserting Him who called you by the grace of Christ, for a different gospel; 7, which is really not another; only there are some who are disturbing you and want to distort the gospel of Christ.*

> 2 Corr. 11: 13, *For such men are false apostles, deceitful workers, disguising themselves as apostles of Christ.*

By late in the first century conditions had grown so dire that false ministers openly refused to receive representatives of the apostles and were excommunicating true Christians from church.

> 3 John 1: 10, *For this reason, if I come, I will call attention to his deeds which he does, unjustly accusing us with wicked words; and not satisfied with this, he himself does not receive the brethren, either, and he forbids those who desire to do so and put them out of the church.*

Enter Constantine, the pagan emperor of Rome, at a time when the church was divided into bitter warring camps. Seeking to unite his empire politically as well as religiously he sanctioned the council of Nicea. The year was (recorded as) 325 AD. The Arian controversy was the primary concern for the church during this time. Arius, a priest from Alexandria in Egypt taught that Christ, because He was the Son of God, must have had a beginning and therefore was a special creation by God. Further if Jesus was the Son, the Father, of necessity must be older. Opposing the teachings of Arius was Athanasius, a deacon from Alexandria also. His view was an early form of Trinitarianism where the Father, Son, and the Holy Spirit, were one in the same, but at the same time distinct from each other.

NOTE: Athanasius probably picked up his trinity ideas from Tertullian, a lawyer and presbyter who hailed from Carthage, Africa. 155 AD – 220 AD. He was noted to be the first to use the word "Trinity" as he put forth the theory of Father, Son, and Spirit were all one being of substance.

As emperor, Constantine was in the usual position of deciding church doctrine even though he was not a Christian.

It is recorded that Constantine actually waited till he was on his death bed to get baptized. So this pagan emperor presided over the Council of Nicea actively guiding discussions from the clergy. With the emperors approval the council rejected the minority view of Arius and approved Athanasius's view of the Trinity. This decision created more instability than it provided. The social unrest often bloody between followers of Arius and the council of Nicea continued until the next council was sanctioned by another Roman emperor, Theodosius. The year was (recorded as) 381 AD and the place was Constantinople. Today Istanbul.

To resolve the ongoing Arian controversy Theodosius appointed Archbishop Gregory of Nazianzus. But Gregory soon became ill and had to withdraw from the council so next in line to be chosen was an elderly city senator, a non-christian called Nectarious.

So a man who was not a Christian and not baptized was appointed to preside over a major church council tasked with determining what the church would teach regarding the nature of God.

The Trinity declaration was affirmed by the council in Constantinople and would become known as the Nicene-Constantinopolitan Creed. Once this decision had been reached the Roman emperor Theodosius would tolerate no dissenting views as he issued has own edict that read:

> *"We now order that all churches are to be handed over to the Bishops who profess Father, Son, and Holy Spirit, of a single majesty, of the same glory of one splendor who establish no difference by sacrilegious separation but (who affirm) the order of the Trinity by recognizing the person and uniting Godhead."*

Later another edict from Theodosius went further in demanding obedience in the form of enforced compliance to the approved teaching of the Trinity.

> *"Let us believe the one deity of the Father, the Son and the Holy Spirit, in equal majesty and in a holy Trinity. We authorize the followers of this law to assume the title of Catholic Christians; but as for the others, since,* in our judgment, they are foolish madmen, *we decree that* they shall be branded with the ignominious name of heretics, *and shall not presume to give their conventicles [assemblies] the name of churches.*
> *"They will suffer in the first place the chastisement of the divine condemnation,* **and the second the punishment which our authority, in accordance with the will of Heaven, shall decide to inflict"**

This is the amazing story of how the doctrine of the Trinity came to be introduced hundreds of years after the bible was written. What this story tells us is from the birth of Jesus Christ to the council of Nicea in 325 AD, the Trinity doctrine was not recognized as biblical and was not taught by Jesus or the Apostles or by the early church itself.

So we understand this doctrine which was invented by the clergy of the Catholic Church had to be developed over decades through trial and error until eventually it was thrust upon the Christian world under forced compliance and those who did not believe in the Trinity were branded heretics worthy of punishment as decided by the empire.

We cannot say we were not warned.

> Acts 20: 29, *I know that after my departure savage wolves will come in among you, not sparing the flock;* 30, *and from among your own selves men will arise, speaking perverse things, to draw away the disciples after them.*

CHAPTER EIGHT

IS GOD OMNIPRESENT AND DOES HE KNOW EVERYTHING ALL THE TIME?

God, the creator of all things great and small. The God we know that was before all things. Is this same God everywhere and knows all things all the time? The title of this chapter will understandably draw an instant negative recoiled reaction from the modern Christian of today but as other things forgotten or hidden from the Christian, this concept also needs to be revealed and understood. This chapter is by no means a belittling or lessening of the greatest entity the world will ever know. But considering the idea of a God that does not know everything all the time; this concept crashes right into its rival action which is the greatest gift man has ever received from God–free will.

And this is my premise. God cannot know everything all the time because it was He who gave us "free will" as evidenced in bible scripture.

> Proverbs 16: 1, *The **plans of the heart belong to man**, But the answer of the tongue is from the LORD.*

> Proverbs 16: 9, *The mind of **man plans his way**, But the LORD directs his steps.*

Matt. 12: 37, *For by your words you will be justified, and **by your words you will be condemned.***"

Gal. 6: 7, *Do not be deceived, God is not mocked; **for whatever a man sows,** this he will also reap*

Joshua 24: 15, *If it is disagreeable in your sight to serve the LORD, **choose for yourselves** today whom you will serve.....*

As the bible tells us, man has the free will to plan his own way, say his own words, sow what he will, and serve whom he chooses. These actions are the consequences of the gift of free will given to man by God. But that being said God says He still knows us does He not? We know He knew us in the spirit world before our birth, but after being born and given the gift of free will we now are somewhat different so then how does He fully know us now? Does He just know us by divine design or does He use a procedure to learn who we are?

Psalms 139: 1, *O LORD, You have **searched** me and **known** me.*

Psalms 139: 23, ***Search** me, O God, and **know my heart**; Try me and know my anxious thoughts;*

Jeremiah 17: 10, *I, the LORD, **search** the heart.....*

1 Sam. 16: 7, *But the LORD said to Samuel, "Do not look at his appearance or at the height of his stature, because I have rejected him; for God sees not as man sees, for man looks at the outward appearance, **but the LORD looks at the heart.**"*

Romans 8: 27, *and **He who searches the hearts knows** what the mind of the Spirit is, because He intercedes for the saints according to the will of God.*

Here God is telling us how He knows the man of free will. **He searches the heart of men to know them.** What this is telling us is God has to do something to know something. He does not say, I already know this guy. What He does say is He will search someones heart to then know them. But you might point to Luke 12: 7, *Indeed, the very hairs of your head are all numbered.* This is a physical action to arrive at a defined answer on a physical part of a man and has nothing to do with mans free will. While God has the ability to know how many hairs are on your head that is not what I am saying because God also said He searches earthly mens hearts to know them.

So the question that comes into focus now is how can God know a person born centuries in the future coming from a line of ancestors who have been given free will?

In Genesis 6, we find God repenting for His creation of man.

> Gen. 6: 5, *Then the LORD saw that the wickedness of man was great on the earth, and that every intent of the thoughts of his heart was only evil continually. 6, The LORD was sorry that He had made man on the earth, and He was grieved in His heart.*

Considering God's state of mind in verse 6, when He said "He was sorry that He made man", God is telling us He made some sort of misjudgment or mistake and His plans did not turn out the way He originally thought they would. Why do we know this?

> Gen. 1: 31, *God saw **"all"** that He had made, and behold, it was very good.....*

Since God told us in Gen. 1, all He created was very good this tells us that at this point in time He had no idea His good creations would later turn out bad as evidenced in Gen. 6: 6.

If God knew ahead of time His creations would turn out bad at some time in the future God would have said something like this in Gen. 1: 31:

1. My creations are good for now.
2. My creations are good but later they will turn out bad.
3. My creations are good but not that good.

We know God is an entity of perfection and would not create something that was designed to be imperfect. When He said His creations were very good, we as Christians are bound to believe Him. But being created perfect is one thing and given the blessing by God of free will is another. Our free will blessing allows us to make mistakes God would not want us to make. It allows us to go down the wrong path that God would not want us to go. We as Christians need to understand the difference between Gods knowledge and mans free will.

We know God can foretell the future in ways because He used prophets to pass on future prophesies to His people. We also know He raises up certain individuals to accomplish His future goals. But there are some events that God tells us He does not know how things will turn out and it must be emphasized that it is "some" of them.

Usually, but not always, two conditions exist that influences a future event that God lets us know He does not know how things will turn out.

1. Mans free will.
2. A very long time must pass before the future event will happen.

Taking the example already discussed into consideration from the creation of the world to Genesis 6, where God tells us He was sorry for creating man, we find that a lot of time had passed. Adding up the 10 generations from Adam to Noah we arrive at approximately 1056 years. But also adding Noah's age of 600 years we now get 1656 years. We already know in scripture that God knows men by reading their hearts but which mans heart can God read that will be not be born until 10 generations in the future? Considering all the men and women in these 10 generations of ancestors were also given free will to choose their own way in the world only further adds to the distortion of trying to know what will happen in the future. So is it fair to God Himself for us to claim He is supposed to know all mens hearts not born yet that He did not have a chance to search?

Considering another story in the bible, did God foresee Eve taking of the forbidden fruit in the Garden of Eden? God did not say "I am telling you Adam and Eve to stay away from the tree of knowledge but I know you are going to break my commandment." In this case Eve exercised what God had given her. Her free will. And then made the decision by all by herself to break Gods commandment.

If we examine the conversation between God and Adam and Eve after the commandment was broken we find the Lord is full of questions that He didn't know the answers to.

> Gen. 3: 9, *Then the LORD God called to the man, and said to him, "Where are you?"*
>
> Gen. 3: 11, *And He said, "Who told you that you were naked? Have you eaten from the tree of which I commanded you not to eat?"*
>
> Gen. 3: 13, *Then the LORD God said to the woman, "What is this you have done?"*

God is not a liar or a deceiver when He asks questions. He is not faking us out into thinking He only asks questions to make the story sound better either. This bible scripture tells us God is asking questions to receive answers to issues He wants to know about.

This is what God did not say in this story.

> Gen. 3: 9, Adam I know where you are.
>
> Gen. 3: 11, I know the serpent told you that you were naked, How come you ate from the tree that I told you not to.
>
> Gen. 3: 13, I know what you did Eve!

If we take this bible story as it was written, the deed Eve did took the Lord by surprise because Eve admits she was told by God not to partake of the forbidden fruit and God does not give commandments He expects people to break or He wouldn't give them in the first place.

In our next example God does not command the Israelites to obey His will. He actually gives them a proposal and then confesses that He does not know if they will accomplish it.

> Ex. 19, 5, *Now then," **if** " you will indeed obey My voice and keep My covenant, then you shall be My own possession among all the peoples, for all the earth is Mine; 6, and **you shall be to Me a kingdom of priests and a holy nation.** ' These are the words that you shall speak to the sons of Israel."*

Here God does not say "I know you will obey me". God lets us know He doesn't know if the Israelites are up to the task. God leaves Moses with an unanswered question.

A yet unfulfilled goal proposed by God that included conditions based on the passing of time, which tells us the outcome was unknowable by God at the time it was proposed. So after many generations had passed we actually find out that the Israelites did indeed make the cut and accomplished the goal God had initially put before Moses in Exodus so long ago.

> 1 Peter 2: 9, ***But you are** A CHOSEN RACE, **A royal PRIESTHOOD, A HOLY NATION**, A PEOPLE FOR God's OWN POSSESSION, so that you may proclaim the excellencies of Him who has called you out of darkness into His marvelous light; 10, **for you once were NOT A PEOPLE**, but "now" you are **THE PEOPLE OF GOD**; you had NOT RECEIVED MERCY, but now you have RECEIVED MERCY.*

So here again, there is no way God could have predicted the outcome of His original request of the Israelites because of the amount of time which had to pass for the conditions He had put forth had not been met. But this is a case of the Israelites exercising their free will to accomplish the goal God put before them. This story is actually much deeper than it appears and some extra discernment by the Christian would be helpful.

Article: biblebro.net God is not everywhere and does not know everything. (no date)

"This Christian idea that God is everywhere and knows everything has over time morphed into a type of personal comfort zone. A crutch to lean on in times of adversity. This idea is sometimes referred to as God's omnipresence. To prove that God is not everywhere all we must do is find one place where He is not. To prove that God does not know everything all we must do is find one thing in scripture that He does not know.

To begin with let us answer the question what is God?

1. He looks like His creation – a man. Gen. 1: 26. *Then God said, "Let Us make man in Our image, according to Our likeness;*
2. God is spirit. John 4: 24, *God is spirit, and those who worship Him must worship in spirit and truth.*

So God has the physical characteristics of a man but is also spirit. When asked where is God, the Christian quickly exclaims "God is everywhere!" But God cannot be everywhere if He tells us the location where he is at.

Question: Is God everywhere?

Matt. 6: 9, *Pray, then, in this way: 'Our Father who is in heaven,*

Psalms 14: 2, *The LORD has looked down from heaven upon the sons of men To see if there are any who understand, Who seek after God.*

> Gen. 11: 5, *The LORD came down to see the city and the tower which the sons of men had built.*

If God says He is in heaven then He is not on earth at that specific time. For the Lord to say He came down to see a city, He must have not been in that city. Lastly, if He was everywhere then verse 5 would have God saying "I am already down there looking at the city." Let us examine the statement: God Searches to find. Why would He have to search for anything if He already is everywhere?

> Gen. 18: 26, *So the LORD said, "**If I find in Sodom fifty righteous within the city, then I will spare the whole place on their account.**"*

Here God is admitting He doesn't know "if" there are 50 righteous people in he city and He is going to have to search the city to find out. If God was everywhere why would He say He has to search? And again, God does give us false statements to make the story sound better.

> Deut. 1: 32, *But for all this, you did not trust the LORD your God,* 33, *who goes before you on your way, to seek out a place for you to encamp, in fire by night and cloud by day, to show you the way in which you should go.*

Here again God tells us He is seeking a place for the Israelites to camp. A God who is everywhere would already know where the tribes should camp. These scriptures listed here tells us God had no foreknowledge of the events He was getting involved in.

Some may point to Proverbs 15, that does say God eyes are everywhere.

> Prov. 15: 3, *The eyes of the LORD are in every place, Watching the evil and the good.*

The book of Isaiah lets us know this type of action is very possible considering Gods location.

> Isaiah 66: 1, *Thus says the LORD, "Heaven is My throne and the earth is My footstool.*

> Isaiah 40: 22, *It is He who sits above the circle of the earth, And its inhabitants are like grasshoppers*

These verses tell us the good Lord is sitting above us watching everything happen so His eyes actually can be described as being everywhere in the remote sense of seeing something like the earth in its entirety from a distance. But it also gives a single location of where God is so it doesn't change the reality of the other bible scripture saying God is not everywhere all the time and must still come down to the earth for a closer look to search for things.

Question: Does God know everything?

This question was basically answered by some of the same verses just listed from the last question.

1. Psalms 14: 2, God had to look down from Heaven to see "if" any understood and who was seeking God.
2. Gen. 11: 5, God had to come down to earth to see the city with the tower of babel and to see what was going on.
3. Gen. 18: 26, God didn't know if there were 50 righteous in Sodom.
4. Deut. 1: 32, God didn't have any foreknowledge of a good camping site for the Israelites.

Some will point to 1 John to find a verse telling us God knows all things.

> 1 John 3: 19, *We will know by this that we are of the truth, and will assure our heart before Him* 20, *in whatever our heart*

condemns us; for God is greater than our heart and knows all things.

These two verses mention the heart three times so we can be confident that this is another scripture showing us God can read our hearts and because of this He can know all things about us.

So what does God know? Everything we as His children see, hear, touch, and smell. He knows these things because He created all things so in that sense He does know everything. Does God <u>not</u> knowing everything during every moment in time because He blessed us with free will, in any way diminish the greatness of the most stunningly brilliant and most powerful entity the world will ever know?

Does Him not being everywhere in all moments in time lessen the praises of the single creator of all things great and small?

Finding the understanding that God gave us the gift of free will which made each person a decision maker and accountable for their own actions causes God to have to search our hearts for answers. But God has the advantage because He has this ability to search our hearts and to know us. Therefore He can acquire the foreknowledge of what we will do before we do it thus giving Him access to our individual future.

> 1 Chron. 28: 9, *As for you, my son Solomon, know the God of your father, and serve Him with a whole heart and a willing mind; for the LORD searches all hearts, and understands every intent of the thoughts.*

CHAPTER NINE

REINCARNATION: THE MISSING LINK IN CHRISTIANITY

We all have heard the stories of people claiming to have been someone else in a previous life. Youtube is full of these stories but usually these claims are from the very young and many times they are dismissed as a vivid imagination. But in history Napoleon told the Papal representatives that in a previous life he was Charlemagne. General George Patton was a firm believer in reincarnation and believed he was the Carthaginian General Hannibal in a previous life. Musician Phil Collins strangely believes he was a defender during the siege of the Alamo in far off San Antonio, Texas. So just what really is this thing called reincarnation.

Reincarnation: Asserts that only through a repeating cycle of death and rebirth is the human soul able to purge itself of sin and evil with the goal of purification from sin to ultimately be worthy of everlasting heavenly peace.

As said before many of the reported reincarnations come from young children when they begin to talk. Sometimes the child will suddenly out of the blue say things like, "where is my real mother?" or

"Why am I here with you?", or "I want to go back to my real mommy." This could be a sign of reincarnation. Again, many times these claims are dismissed as a young childs wild imagination but when the childs claims become persistent and research of their specific claims proves to have validity then the idea of imagination transforms into the idea of reincarnation.

Example 1: The strange case of a four year old who recalled a previous life as a Hollywood Agent.

"In 2009 four year old Ryan Hammons began waking up clutching his chest and screaming about how his heart exploded in Hollywood. His mother Cyndi became intrigued when Ryan revealed more details from a former life. He insisted he once lived in a house in Hollywood on a street with the name "**rock**" in it where he had three sons and a friend named "**Senator Fives.**" One day Cyndi was going through a book featuring photos from old Hollywood. Ryan peeked over her shoulder and excitedly identified one man as George and another as himself. One of the men in the photo was film star George Raft and the other man was Martin Martyn who died in 1964. Upon contacting Martins daughter, she confirmed that her father, Martin was a Hollywood agent who lived on North **Roxbury** Drive, and had three sons and once met with New York **Senator, Irving Ives.** After the meeting with Martyns daughter Ryan lost interest in his Hollywood memories. He told his mother afterward his daughters energy had changed. Upon seeing people from their past have moved on, children who claim to be reincarnated many times receive closure and forget their former existence."

Example 2, James Leiningers past life as a fighter pilot.

"James was 2 ½ years old when he starting talking about his vivid dreams and strong memories of being a man called Lt. James McCready Huston. He said he had been a WWII fighter pilot from Union Town, Pennsylvania, who had been killed at Iwo Jima more than 50 years before. At two years old the boy began talking about aviation and his knowledge of the subject was amazing. He hadn't learned about flying or being in the Airforce from his parents as they knew nothing about flying. James would have nightmares and would scream "airplane crash, on fire, can't get out, help." James went on to tell his parents he had flown a plane called a Corsair which took off from a boat called The Natoma. James parents decided to do some research and discovered that there had been an escort carrier called the Natoma Bay, which had been in the battle of Iwo Jima and indeed there had been a pilot called James Huston who's plane had been shot down on March 3, 1945. James Huston's cousin Bob now 74, said "its amazing that every thing the boy said was exactly the account told to James Hustons father and also my mother. There is no way this child could have known that."

Example 3, Edgar Cayce (1877 – 1945)

"Known as the sleeping prophet and is widely considered to be the most documented and accurate psychic in the world. As a true believer in Christ, the boy Edgar Cayce one day prayed to God and said that he wanted to help others, especially sick children. He later claimed to have had a vision that convinced him that his prayers would be answered. As an adult and a practicing psychic Cayce would go into a trance and reveal cures for people. It was in these trances that Cayce announced he had been reincarnated throughout history and claimed to have been an Atlantean from the lost continent of Atlantis. Because this humble Sunday school teachers predictions and statements regarding his visions of the past and future would prove to be extremely accurate during the course of his lifetime, the belief in reincarnation was given much substance and legitimacy.

Today when conversing with the Christian over the possibility of reincarnation he will immediately zero in on Hebrews 9.

> Hebrews 9: 27, *And inasmuch as it is appointed for men to die once and after this* comes j*udgment,*

This one verse settles it in the Christians mind. The bible says right there in Hebrews 9, men die only once does it not? But if that one verse ends all discussion on the subject of reincarnation then what about that guy Lazarus? Seems he did die once but someone changed all that didn't they?

> John 11: 38, *So Jesus, again being deeply moved within, came to the tomb. Now it was a cave, and a stone was lying against it.* 39, *Jesus *said, "Remove the stone." Martha, the sister of the deceased, said to Him, "Lord, by this time there will be a stench, for he has been* dead *four days.*
> 40, *Jesus *said to her, "Did I not say to you that if you believe, you will see the glory of God?"* 41, *So they removed the stone. Then Jesus raised His eyes, and said, "Father, I thank You that You have heard Me.* 42. *"I knew that You always hear Me; but because of the people standing around I said it, so that they may believe that You sent Me."* 43, *When He had said these things, He cried out with a loud voice, "Lazarus, come forth."* 44, *The man who had died came forth, bound hand and foot with wrappings, and his face was wrapped around with a cloth. Jesus *said to them, "Unbind him, and let him go."*

So is the story of Lazarus a direct contradiction of this claim in Hebrews that men are appointed to die only once? Looking further into this appointed death business we find more bible stories in direct contradiction to Hebrews 9: 27, also.

> 1 Kings 17: 17, *Now it came about after these things that the son of the woman, the mistress of the house, became sick; and his sickness was so severe that there was no breath left in him.* 18, *So she said to Elijah, "What do I have to do with you, O man of God? You have come to me to bring my iniquity to remembrance and to put my son to death!"* 19, *He said to her, "Give me your son." Then he took him from her bosom and carried him up to the upper room where he was living, and laid him on his own bed.* 20, *he called to the LORD and said, "O LORD my God, have You also brought calamity to the widow with whom I am staying, by causing her son to die?"* 21, *Then he stretched himself upon the child three times, and called to the LORD and said, "O LORD my God, I pray You, let this child's life return to him."* 22, *The LORD heard the voice of Elijah, and the life of the child returned to him and he revived.*

> 2 Kings 13: 20. *Elisha died, and they buried him. Now the bands of the Moabites would invade the land in the spring of the year.* 21. *As they were burying a man, behold, they saw a marauding band; and they cast the man into the grave of Elisha. And when the man touched the bones of Elisha he revived and stood up on his feet.*

> Luke 7: 11, *Soon afterwards He went to a city called Nain; and His disciples were going along with Him, accompanied by a large crowd.* 12, *Now as He approached the gate of the city, a dead man was being carried out, the only son of his mother, and she was a widow; and a sizeable crowd from the city was with her.* 13, *When the Lord saw her, He felt compassion for her, and said to her, "Do not weep."* 14, *And He*

came up and touched the coffin; and the bearers came to a halt. And He said, "Young man, I say to you, arise!" 15, *The dead man sat up and began to speak. And* Jesus *gave him back to his mother.*

Luke 8: 49, *While He was still speaking, someone *came from* the house of *the synagogue official, saying, "Your daughter has died; do not trouble the Teacher anymore."*
50, *But when Jesus heard* this, *He answered him, "Do not be afraid* any longer; *only believe, and she will be made well."* 51, *When He came to the house, He did not allow anyone to enter with Him, except Peter and John and James, and the girl's father and mother.* 52, *Now they were all weeping and lamenting for her; but He said, "Stop weeping, for she has not died, but is asleep."*n 53, *And they* began *laughing at Him, knowing that she had died.* 54, *He, however, took her by the hand and called, saying, "Child, arise!"* 55, *And her spirit returned, and she got up immediately; and He gave orders for* something *to be given her to eat.* 56, *Her parents were amazed; but He instructed them to tell no one what had happened.*

Acts 9: 37, *Now in Joppa there was a disciple named Tabitha (which translated* in Greek *is called Dorcas); this woman was abounding with deeds of kindness and charity which she continually did.* 38, *And it happened at that time that she fell sick and died; and when they had washed her body, they laid it in an upper room.* 39, *Since Lydda was near Joppa, the disciples, having heard that Peter was there, sent two men to him, imploring him, "Do not delay in coming to us."* 40, *So Peter arose and went with them. When he arrived, they brought him into the upper room; and all the widows stood beside him, weeping and showing all the tunics and garments that Dorcas used to make while she was with them.* 41, *But Peter sent*

> *them all out and knelt down and prayed, and turning to the body, he said, "Tabitha, arise." And she opened her eyes, and when she saw Peter, she sat up. 42, And he gave her his hand and raised her up; and calling the saints and widows, he presented her alive.*
>
> Acts 20: 9, *And there was a young man named Eutychus sitting on the window sill, sinking into a deep sleep; and as Paul kept on talking, he was overcome by sleep and fell down from the third floor and was picked up dead. 10, But Paul went down and fell upon him, and after embracing him, he said, "Do not be troubled, for his life is in him." 11, When he had gone* back *up and had broken the bread and eaten, he talked with them a long while until daybreak, and then left. 12, They took away the boy alive, and were greatly comforted.*

Here we have 7 people who all missed their one appointment to die just once. So taking the bible as a whole there seems to be a developing problem with understanding this die once statement in Hebrews 9: 27.

If we look at the entire chapter of Hebrews 9, it is not talking about appointments to die. It is discussing the comparison of the first covenant in the Old Testament and the new covenant in the New Testament with Jesus. Verse 27 is used to help qualify the larger idea of Christ having to die only once to complete the blood covenant.

Even today one quick search on Youtube on the subject of death experiences and you will see a large range of stories of people claiming to have died and come back.

Since the bible in five books clearly and repeatedly refutes the Hebrews 9: 27, claim of man being appointed to die only once I believe I can say with much confidence we are dealing with a misunderstanding or a mistranslation of this bible verse. Consider the idea that a man can be appointed to die once in his life but as the bible has shown our Lord is a God of miracles is He not? Just because someone has an appointment that doesn't mean they have to keep it. What about Enoch and Elijah? They qualified as men didn't they and they never even showed up for their appointments. I think leaving verse 27 as a qualifier for the larger story of Christs dying once for one blood sacrifice is more appropriate for understanding Hebrews 9. This chapter clearly has nothing to do with reincarnation. The larger story of Christs dying once for one blood sacrifice is more appropriate for Hebrews 9.

If you are curious if the bible talks about reincarnation let your curiosity settle on the story of John the Baptist.

> Luke 1: 13, *But the angel said to him, "Do not be afraid, Zacharias, for your petition has been heard, and your wife Elizabeth will bear you a son, and you will give him the name John.*

> Luke 1: 17, *It is he who will go* as a forerunner *before Him in the **spirit** and power of Elijah, TO TURN THE HEARTS OF THE FATHERS BACK TO THE CHILDREN, and the disobedient to the attitude of the righteous, so as to make ready a people prepared for the Lord."*

This verse is not a describing a football game with the use of the word "spirit" and not to be confused with the slang terminology used for spirit today. The bibles use of the word spirit is telling us that this child yet to be born will have the "spirit" of Elijah, or, Elijah's spirit will be reborn in the new body that will be named John. For more clarity on this story we will receive it from Jesus Himself.

> Matt. 11: 14, *And if you are willing to accept* it, *John himself is Elijah who was to come.*

This should be the end of it. Christ Himself just confirmed it. John is the reincarnation of Elijah so said the living Christ. But naysayers will dismiss Christs own words and point to John 1.

> John 1: 19, *This is the testimony of John, when the Jews sent to him priests and Levites from Jerusalem to ask him, "Who are you?"* 20, *And he confessed and did not deny, but confessed, "I am not the Christ."* 21, *They asked him, "What then?* **Are you Elijah?" And he said, "I am not."** *"Are you the Prophet?" And he answered, "No."* 22. *Then they said to him, "Who are you, so that we may give an answer to those who sent us? What do you say about yourself?"* 23, **He said, "I am A VOICE OF ONE CRYING IN THE WILDERNESS, 'MAKE STRAIGHT THE WAY OF THE LORD,' as Isaiah the prophet said."**

Yes there are actual Christians in the world today that will take John's word over Christs as to who John says he really is. But if you look a little deeper into John 1, you will find that while John is not claiming to be Elijah, he is also not even claiming to be John the Baptist. He says he is a *voice crying in the wilderness.* He is using a metaphor to describe himself at the time of this inquiry of who he is.

If Christs claim of who John is, is not convincing enough we will look to the Old Testament book of Malachi for even more confirmation.

> Malachi 4: 5, *Behold,* ***I am going*** *to send you Elijah the prophet before the coming of the great and terrible day of the LORD.*

You will notice God is talking in the future tense as He says He is "going" to send Elijah before Christ comes. We know that Elijah was a prophet way back in 1 Kings. So by the time the book of Malachi was written Elijah was long gone. Malachi 4, is obviously a prophesy of a future event yet to come. Long gone Elijah is going to make a re-appearance here on earth and this re-entering the world by Elijah was accomplished by his reincarnation into John the Baptist confirmed by Christ Himself. The next statement by Christ Himself is:

Matt. 11: 14, *And if you are willing to accept* it, *John himself is Elijah who was to come.* 15, **He who has ears to hear, let him hear.**

So do you count yourself among those who have ears to hear?

What of the atheists argument against the Christian religion? They will say, "how can some poor black kid dying on some hill in Africa never knowing your Christ go to hell? What did he do wrong?" Inserting reincarnation into the equation you will come up with a reasonable and believable answer to the Atheists concern.

"Living multiple lives this child will eventually arrive at a time when the Christian missionaries are visiting his village bringing the good news of Christ. At this point in his life this same child, or now adult, in some remote village in Africa can now exercise his free will to accept the gospel of Christ."

Its the same process and conclusion for the infant or toddler dying early in life. Under the concept of one life and one death we are left with the question of how many thousands of years of people on earth died not knowing Christ? How can they be saved? So how about another life? How about another chance to receive the gospel of Christ at some point later in the future?

Reincarnation fits perfectly into Gods plan of His missionaries spreading the gospel to the world and eventually reaching all people over the span of centuries.

In the early turbulent years of the church one of the original church fathers was Origen. 185 AD – 254 AD. He is famous for composing his seminal work on Christian Theology called: "On First Principles" which on one point argues for a complex form of reincarnation wherein the soul inhabits multiple bodies whether physical or spiritual over the course of time. The politics revolving around the Origen heresy began when a powerful group of Cardinals and Bishops convinced the current Roman emperor Justinian, that it was not in the best interests of the empire to allow Origins writings to be continued being copied and distributed. Their reasoning behind this was explained that if every soul had once pre-existed with God, then Christ wasn't anything special to have come from God. And if his (Justinians) subjects realized they also were the children of God they might begin to believe they no longer needed an emperor, or needed to pay taxes, or needed to obey the Catholic Church. So as the Catholic Church during the early years was actively reining in heretics, Origin was no exception. Two hundred years after his death the clergy were finally successful by the Second Council of Constantinople in 553 where Origen was finally and officially cleansed from the church. His critics attacked his views on the idea of reincarnation on five points.

1. It seems to minimize Christian salvation.
2. It is in conflict with the resurrection of the body.
3. It creates an unnatural separation between body and soul.
4. It is built on a much too speculative use of Christian scripture.
5. There is no recollection of previous lives.

So the early biblical concept of reincarnation advocated by Origen was stamped out by the Catholic Church for two reasons"

1. Money
2. Power

If we take one step sideways into a book called the Septuagint, we find an odd addition in the book of Job that seems to have not been able to find its way into the KJV or the NASB versions of the bible. The Septuagint is Latin for seventy, as in the 70 translators of this version of the bible which is the earliest existing Greek translation of the Hebrew bible and dates in the 3rd century BC, often called – The Apostles bible. Comparing bible verses we first look into the NASB and the KJV:

NASB: Job: 42: 17, *And Job died, an old man and full of days.*

> KJV: Job: 42: 17, *So Job died, being old and full of days.*

But in the Septuagint we find this:

> The Septuagint: Job 42: 17, *And job died an old man and full of days,* **and it is written that he will rise again with those whom the Lord raises up…….**

Then the verses goes into a detailed explanation of Job who is described in the Syriac book as living in the land of Ausis which borders Idumea and his name before was Jobab.

So one should wonder why these extra verses in Job 42 in the Septuagint were omitted from the later versions of the KJV and NASB bible translations. Did Job know something that was a little too close to Origins heretical views? Was this part of the book of Job paralleling what Jesus said about John being Elijah? Searching other scriptures in the book of Job we find other interesting messages that give weight to the claim of another life in Job 42: 17.

> Job 1: 21, *Then Job arose and tore his robe and shaved his head, and he fell to the ground and worshiped.* 21, **He said,"Naked I came from my mother's womb, And naked I shall return there....**

It seems pretty clear that Job is saying here that he believes he is going to end up being born again at some future point in time. Then there is this.

> Job 14: 14, *"If a man dies, will he live* again? *All the days of my struggle I will wait Until my change comes.*

It sounds like in Job 14, Job is answering his own question. He will wait until the changing of his current life into another life comes. But the same verse of Job 14, in The Septuagint leaves us with an even clearer view of what Job is saying.

> Septuagint: Job 14: 14, *For if a man should die, shall he live again, having accomplished the days of his life? I will wait till I exist again* (?)

It was I who put parenthesis around the question mark in this verse 14 because it is obviously added by the later translators of the Septuagint because the last sentence of verse 14 is not a question. It is a clear statement by Job admitting that he will exist again in another life. So it seems the translators of the book of Job in the NASB and the KJV bibles have been busy with their own corrections as they actively worked to mangle the Septuagints book of Job to reflect their own sanitized version. But doing the research we can see Job is telling us he has an understanding of reincarnation as it relates to his life outlined in the bible book bearing his name.

Are there other hidden verses pointing to reincarnation in other bible books that escaped the translation sanitizers pen?

> Hebrews 11: 35, *Women received* back *their dead by resurrection; and others were tortured, not accepting their release, so that they might obtain a better resurrection;*

Here we have the word "resurrection" used twice to explain the expectation of another life.

Free Dictionary.com: Definition of "resurrection."
  a. The act of restoring a dead person, for example, to life.
  b. The condition of having been restored to life.

This verse in Hebrews 11, says these women will get back their dead by having them restored to life. Chapter 11 in Hebrews is about several biblical events covering faith. It outlines how many have died in faith. This story is not a Jesus/Lazarus raising from the dead resurrection event as verse 13 in this chapter says: *All these died in faith, without receiving the promises. Looking at Hebrews 11: 35, through reincarnation we see that these women will be reunited with their dead husbands, and/or fathers, and/or sons, through a future restored or resurrected new life.* While in the next sentence of verse 35, the "others" were not accepting their release so they could to obtain some sort of blessing or advantage when got restored or resurrected to another future life. Both the women and the others in Hebrews 11 are talking about reincarnation.

Finally in Revelations we find this.

> Rev. 3: 12, **He who overcomes, I will make him a pillar in the temple** *of My God,* **and he will not go out from it anymore;** *and I will write on him the name of My God, and the name of the city of My God, the new Jerusalem, which comes down out of heaven from My God, and My new name. 13 'He who has an ear, let him hear what the Spirit says to the churches.'*

He who overcomes will not go out anymore. Or looking at this verse through reincarnation: He who overcomes their multiple lives tests and trials needed to graduate will not have to be born again and will obtain the promise of everlasting life in heaven. So tell me. Is a 1st grader fit to graduate High-school? Has a plumber learned his trade in a week? Is a doctor an expert surgeon after his first surgery? Can we truly believe as Gods children we have learned all life's lessons needed to dwell with Christ in heaven as a perfect soul in just one life?

Understanding how the concept of reincarnation can influence your future lives.

Here I will outline four stories on how reincarnation "could" influence your future lives. It should be clear that I am not claiming to be the last word on this issue because I am not God who is the ultimate decision maker. These four stories are speculative in nature and should be taken with that frame of reference. The gender involved in these stores will be male as the male carries the bloodline of the father as the female leaves and cleaves to another man.

1. The kind spiritual parents have a son: The mother takes all measures to ensure a healthy son is born. He is brought up in a loving environment and taught and disciplined to respect God and all things spiritual. His parents both set a good moral example for him. He is given a good education to ensure his success. His parents are influential with his selection of a wife. He inherits his fathers wealth.

a) Will this father want to be reborn in his sons future family line?

b) Does this father deserve to be reborn in his sons future family line?

c) Would a just God believe this father earned the right to be reborn in his sons future family line?

2. The disrespectful non-spiritual parents have a son: This man and woman have a son in a careless way causing possible health issues for the baby boy. The child is not taught to be respectful and is raised in a dysfunctional environment. The parents set a bad moral example for the child and offer no spiritual guidance or development. This son grows up disrespectful as he was raised and runs off with a woman. He gets her pregnant and eventually leaves her to raise his son.

a) Will this father want to be reborn in his sons future family line?

b) Does this father deserve to be reborn in his sons future family line?

c) Would a just God believe this father earned the right to be reborn in his sons future family line?

3. The soldier who believes in reincarnation: A war has begun. This soldier has a wife and a son at home. He knows he must fight to save his country from invasion and destruction. He and many of his comrades sacrifice their lives to save their country and ultimately his wife and his sons lives.

d) Will this soldier's son, now because of his sacrifice eventually have a future family line he can be reborn into?

b) Will this soldier be able to be reborn in his country that was saved by his sacrifice?

c) Would a just God believe this father earned the right to be reborn in his sons future family line and also into his original country of birth?

4. The mixed race parents have a son: Their future lives will now be influenced by two different racial bloodlines. If the parents of the mixed race couple encouraged and/or accepted the mixed race child as their own they also could be influencing their future lives with another racial bloodline.

Do you think I am doing a bit of reaching in regards to pointing out one can influence their future lives by what they do in their current life? One more look at Hebrews 11:35 will let you know I am reaching as far a some of the people in that book are

Hebrews 11:35, *Women received back their dead by resurrection; and others were tortured, not accepting their release, so that they might obtain a better resurrection*;

One just might be coming away with the idea that I am a believer in you reap what you sow. Well the reason I am that type of believer is someone else told me to believe that way.

Galatians 6: 7, *Do not be deceived, God is not mocked; for whatever a man sows, this he will also reap.*

Again, it was Christ Himself that told us John the Baptist was Elijah. Should not that be enough for the believing Christian to know that if Elijah came back in another life so could we? Reincarnation is the only rational way to explain spiritual development.

CHAPTER TEN

FLAT EARTH: WHO KNOWS THE STORY? THE CREATOR OR THE CREATED?

Going back in history many ancient cultures believed in a flat earth. From Asia to Norway to even the Greeks until Pythagoras, the Ionian Greek philosopher in the 6th century BC stated that the earth was actually spherical and promptly passed that thought on down to another Greek Aristotle, who himself passed it on down to the Roman Ptolemy. By the first century AD Pliny the elder was in a position to claim that everyone now agreed on the spherical shape of the earth. But in this day and age making the claim that the earth is flat brings chuckles from the atheist, sneers from the scientific community, and condemnation from the Church. I fully understand the atheists reason why he laughs at this view. He hates anything about religion anyway. The scientific community has the need to protect their skeletons in the closet so no surprise there. But I must admit I am perplexed on why the Church seems so adamant in their public disapproval and even condemnation of this view. They downright have shown that they have no interest in even considering this possibility. So this is what I am going to focus this chapter on. The religious view of flat earth. My reasoning for this is that the work on the scientific, historic, geographic, and secular aspects of this subject have already been fully researched and written about.

Meet author Edward Hendrie. He has written two of the finest researched, well thought out, unequaled in comparison, books on the subject of – The Flat Earth.

Book 1. The Greatest Lie on Earth
Book 2. The Sphere of Influence

This body of work is unmatched in the literary world with regards to this subject. No geographical stone is left unturned. No scientific claim or mathematical equation is left unchallenged. All serious related questions on this subject are dismantled point for point as Hendrie pulls back the wizards curtain for all to witness. Book 1, goes into deep details on the religious scripture of the flat earth, the science of why a spherical earth could never be, and the history of the powers behind the invention of the so called blue marble earth. Book 2, lets the whole world know just who is participating in the cover-up. Naming names, Hendrie shines the light on those complicit in the conspiracy of the greatest lie on earth.

Questions such as these and much more are all answered in Hendrie's books.

1. Visibility of distant objects over water.
2. Architectural testimony of buildings, bridges, and train tracks.
3. Airplane flight patterns.
4. NASA photos of the so called blue marble globe examined.
5. NASA moon missions.
6. Google Earths non-globe.
7. Astronomy of the stars explained.
8. Time lapse trickery.
9. Gravity defined.
10. Einsteins role in the globular earth science.

So choose understanding or choose to keep covering your eyes to reality. This work has been completed for all to witness.

****

…..So there once was a man who was a truthseeker. A man known far and wide for spending his time in pursuit of the truth in all things. One day he was approached by a Christian.

Christian: Hello friend, would you like to hear about the good news of Jesus Christ?

Truthseeker: Well, he said stepping back a little. I have looked into your religion a little so would you mind if I asked you a few questions first?

Christian: Not at all.

Truthseeker: The God of your bible says He uses the earth as His footstool and is looking down on us as little grasshoppers. Is that true?

(Acts 7: 49 & Isa. 40: 22)

Christian: Well now. we both know the earth is rotating around the sun at about 60,000 mph while spinning around somewhere in the neighborhood of 1000 mph. I would say its kind of difficult for the earth to be a foot stool at that speed ya think? I mean we know the earth is rotating around the sun in empty space. That's just a metaphor about the footstool. Heaven is trillions of miles away and that is where you will find God.

Truthseeker: Hmm. No footstool for your God and He's not up there looking down at us like grasshoppers. Okay, next question. The God of your bible says that He propped up the earth on pillars correct?

(Job 9: 6 & Ps. 75: 3)

Christian: I think if that was actually the case I am sure we would have heard about those pillars from our friends in Australia. Just another metaphor.

Truthseeker: Hmm, so your God didn't do that either. Okay, but is it not true that in your bible, in the book of Joshua to be exact, that your God said He stopped the sun from moving?

(Josh. 10: 12–14)

Christian: I think we both can agree that the sun is in the middle of the solar system in a stationary position. I mean science has proven this friend. What Joshua obviously saw was the earth had actually stopped making it only look to Joshua like the sun had stopped.

Truthseeker: But thats not what the God of your bible said. He clearly said it was He who stopped the sun from moving and not the earth.

Christian: People back then could not understand things as we can today so they did the best they could when describing what they saw. It was the Earth that was stopped. So, can I tell you about Jesus Christ?

Truthseeker: Uh, thats okay, You've already told me all I need to know.

And there you have it. The Christian spends his entire life denying Gods own account about how His creation came to be, while at the same time professing to be a bible believing follower of the Christian God. So when someone seeking the truth about God is told by the Christian NOT to believe what God is saying about His creation, just who are we to believe? The Christian or God?

It must be said that throughout the entire bible there is not one verse validating or even recognizing the concept of a spherical earth. While the earth is not called specifically "flat" either, the language in the bible that is used to describe the earth expresses the claim in many different ways that the earth is indeed flat.

Argument 1: The earth is stationary.

Referencing the Heliocentric (sun in the center) solar system, science says the earth is hurling through space at 66,600 mph while spinning in orbit at about 1000 mph.

But God tells us the earth is stationary and that it doesn't move at all.

Psalms 93:1, *The LORD reigns, He is clothed with majesty; The LORD has clothed and girded Himself with strength; Indeed, the world is firmly established, it will not be moved.*

Psalms 96: 10, *Say among the nations, "The LORD reigns; Indeed, the world is firmly established, it will not be moved;.....*

Psalms 104: 5, *He established the earth upon its foundations, So that it will not totter forever and ever.*

1 Chron. 16:30, *Tremble before Him, all the earth; Indeed, the world is firmly established, it will not be moved.*

So how can an earth that is firmly established on its foundations to the point that it can NOT be moved, be spinning through space at over 66,000 mph? So who do you believe is telling the truth? The creator or the created?

Argument 2: The Earth is set on pillars.

Job 9: 6, *Who shakes the earth out of its place, And its pillars tremble;*

Psalms 75: 3, *The earth and all who dwell in it melt; It is I who have firmly set its pillars.*

Psalms 104:5, *He raises the poor from the dust, He lifts the needy from the ash heap to make them sit with nobles, And inherit a seat of honour; For the pillars of the earth are the LORD'S, And He set the world on them.*

To get around this scripture the Christian will tell you that its all metaphorical. But where is the reasoning for a metaphor?

Definition of a Metaphor: A metaphor is a figure of speech that describes one thing by saying it is another unlike thing.

Examples of a metaphorical sentence:

1. You are my sunshine
2. She has a heart of gold.
3. You are an angel.
4. She was an angry rattlesnake.

So looking at those listed bible verses one can clearly see there is no comparison being done in them. There is no hidden story here. This is clearly a repeating statement by God and not a metaphorical comparison. When God tells us the earth is set on pillars he is not a using a metaphor any way you look at it.

Argument 3: The earth, sun, moon, and stars are set in the Firmament.

The biblical account of creation in Genesis refutes the commonly held view of a spherical earth that is surrounded by a vacuum of space.

God tells us He put the earth, the sun, the moon, and the stars, in a firmament.

Online Dictionary: Firmament – a vault or "expanse" of the heavens. Viewed as something solid and abiding in the region of the air.

NOTE: The KJV uses the word "firmament" and the NASB uses the word "expanse". Both are the same thing as the Online dictionary explains.

This firmament is a type of solid tent like vault over the skies and the earth.

> Gen. 1: 14, T*hen God said, "Let there be lights **in the expanse** (firmament) **of the heavens** to separate the day from the night, and let them be for signs and for seasons and for days and years;* 15, *and let them be for lights in the expanse of the heavens to give light on the earth"; and it was so.* **16, God made the two great lights, the greater light to govern the day, and the lesser light to govern the night; He made the stars also.** **17, God placed them in the expanse** (firmament) *of the heavens to give light on the earth....*

You will notice that in verses 16 and 17 God tells us He placed the sun, and the moon, and the stars IN the expanse or firmament which is a type of solid mass vault above these lights in the sky while also covering the earth.

Biblical descriptions of Gods firmament:

> Job 37: 18, *Can you, with Him, spread out the skies,* **Strong as a molten mirror?**

> Isa. 40: 22, *It is He who sits above the circle of the earth, And its inhabitants are like grasshoppers,* **Who stretches out the heavens like a curtain And spreads them out like a tent to dwell in.**

> Psalms 104: 2, *Covering Yourself with light as with a cloak,* **Stretching out heaven like a tent curtain.**

So what we are getting from Gods description of the firmament is its a strong solid tent like object that is spread out over the earth and skies while holding within it the earth, sun, moon, and stars.

Argument 4: The earth is in the shape of a circle, not a ball.

> Prov. 8: 27, *When He established the heavens, I was there, When He inscribed* ***a circle*** *on the face of the deep,*

> Job 26: 10, *He has inscribed* ***a circle on the surface of the waters*** *At the boundary of light and darkness.*

> Isa. 40: 22, *It is He who sits above* ***the circle of the earth****, And its inhabitants are like grasshoppers, Who stretches out the heavens like a curtain And spreads them out like a tent to dwell in.*

128 • STEVE GARRETT

Isaiah 40, is a clear description of what the earth with its oceans placed in the firmament looks like. Now here is where the Christian will claim no one at that time in biblical history understood what the earth really looked like so they would use the word "circle" to describe what really was a "ball." Basically they are saying people back then did not know the difference between a circle and a ball.

> Isa. 22: 18, And *roll you tightly **like a ball**,* To be cast *into a vast country.....*

So in biblical times this verse tells us they did know the difference between a circle and a ball back then. A circle is not a ball. A circle is two dimensional and flat. A globe is a three dimensional ball. The two cannot be confused with each other. Have you ever tried to play baseball with a circle?

Argument 5: The earth has corners.

> Isa. 11: 12, *And He will lift up a standard for the nations And assemble the banished ones of Israel, And will gather the dispersed of Judah From **the four corners of the earth.***

> Rev. 7: 1, *After this I saw four angels standing at **the four corners of the earth**.....*

> Rev. 20: 7, *When the thousand years are completed, Satan will be released from his prison,* 8, *and will come out to deceive the nations which are in **the four corners of the earth**.....*

The question these scriptures place before us is, has anyone ever seen the corner of a ball? But here is where the Christian thinks he has an "aha" moment. If I as the author of this book you are now reading just pointed out that the earth is a circle then how can it also have corners? Well, as we all know the land masses of the earth are surrounded by water correct? Therefore it should be easy to understand the "earth" i.e. the above surface land masses can have corners while being within a circle of the larger ocean.

Argument 6: The earth has ends.

> Job 28: 24, *For He looks to the ends of the earth And sees everything under the heavens.*

> Job 37: 3, *Under the whole heaven He lets it loose, And His lightning to the **ends of the earth**.*

> Jer. 16: 13, *LORD, my strength and my stronghold, And my refuge in the day of distress, To You the nations will come From **the ends of the earth** and say.....*

The next question arises. Has anyone ever seen the end of a ball? This claim that the earth has an end by itself could be viewed as some sort of parable or metaphor, but coupled with the claim that the earth has land mass corners within the greater circle of the oceans draws a conclusive picture of a flat earth with a defined end.

Considering Gods biblical description of His creation of earth we arrive at the following conclusions.

1. A flat earth can be in the shape of a circle with its surrounding oceans.
2. A flat earth can have corners on the land mass surfaces.
3. A flat earth will eventually have an end to it.

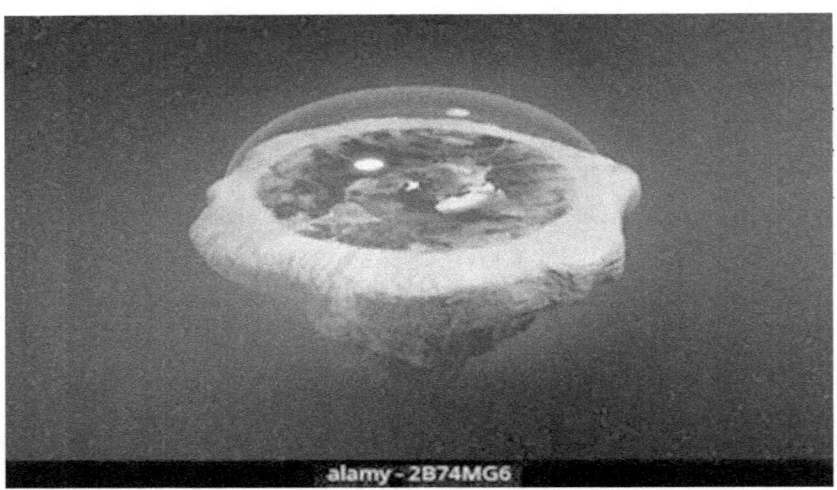

It is God who tells us in the bible that the earth cannot be moved and it is the sun and the moon that rotates in a circular motion inside the firmament above the earth. We already saw that God made the claim it was He who stopped THE SUN and the moon from rotating in Joshua 10, at the request of Joshua.

> Josh. 10: 12, *Then Joshua spoke to the LORD in the day when the LORD delivered up the Amorites before the sons of Israel, and he said in the sight of Israel, "O sun, stand still at Gibeon, And O moon in the valley of Aijalon." 13, **So the sun stood still**, and the moon stopped, Until the nation avenged themselves of their enemies. Is it not written in the book of Jashar? **And the sun stopped in the middle of the sky** and did not hasten to go down for about a whole day. 14, There was no day like that before it or after it, when the LORD listened to the voice of a man; for the LORD fought for Israel.*

For the Christian to dismiss this bible scripture as truth in the book of Joshua, he must:

1. Not believe Joshua when he called on the Lord to stop the sun.
2. Not believe the bible scripture when it clearly records the event of the sun indeed stopping.
3. Not believe the Lord when it was He who said HE stopped the sun.

This is not the only time in the bible the Lord influenced the movement of the sun at the request of His prophets.

> 2 Kings 20: 8, *Now Hezekiah said to Isaiah, "What will be the sign that the LORD will heal me, and that I shall go up to the house of the LORD the third day?"* 9, *Isaiah said, "This shall be the sign to you from the LORD, that the LORD will do the thing that He has spoken: shall the shadow go forward ten steps or go back ten steps?* 10, *So Hezekiah answered, "It is easy for the shadow to decline ten steps; no, but let the shadow turn backward ten steps."* 11, **Isaiah the prophet cried to the LORD, and He brought the shadow on the stairway back ten steps by which it had gone down on the stairway of Ahaz**

Does this scripture mention anything about stopping the earth from moving? It should be clear what causes shadows? Light. There was no mention of someone walking around with a lamp so it should be understood that God caused the sun to move its shadow back ten steps.

There are more than 60 verses in 28 books of the bible which say that it is the sun moving and not one verse telling us it is the earth that is in orbit around the sun.

Looking in Matthew 4, we find the devil taking Jesus to a very high mountain to show him all the kingdoms of the world.

> Matt. 4: 8, *Again, the devil took Him to a very high mountain and showed Him all the kingdoms of the **world** and their*

glory; 9, and he said to Him, "All these things I will give You, if You fall down and worship me."

Here the flat earther can say it would be impossible to see all the kingdoms of the earth if it was a ball. Two points come into play here.

1. If the earth was flat then just maybe Jesus who is a God with supernatural powers and satan who has the ranking of an archangel also with supernatural powers could possibly see all the kingdoms of the whole world if it was flat.
2. Strongs Concordance definitions for the biblical Hebrew word "Erets" is:
   a) Earth
   b) **Land**
   c) World

So choosing the second description of the biblical Hebrew word "erets" satan could have easily been showing Jesus the all kingdoms of the "land" from a high point on a mountain making this bible verse a realistic probability on a flat earth.

So what about Antarctica? Since it doesn't exist there really is nothing about it. In the center of the earth is the North Pole. The earth continues to spread out across the flat disk until it reaches a tall ice wall circle that surrounds the oceans.

A BRIDGE OVER THE SINS OF YOUR FATHERS • 133

This region called Antarctica seems to be a place of intrigue for the conspiracy minded. This cold place has been protected since 1959 by a World Treaty which states no single entity can take possession or lay claim to any part of Antarctica. So that means whats beyond that ice wall remains a mystery.

Article: New York Times, 10/20/1985 – 16 areas restricted under the Antarctica Treaty.

> "A 32 nation group of countries agreed to restrict human access to 16 areas of environmental value in Antarctica. The

> Treaty's decision to limit access to 13 special scientific zones and 3 environmental areas which represents a 75 % increase in such restricted areas."

Citing online sources the written consensus is anyone can travel to Antarctica anytime. Wikipedia and Google agree with this consensus. So meet one, Frederick Dodson who actually tried to test that theory.

Article: Realitycreation.org. 11/2/2021 Excerpt from the book: Mysteries of the Arctic and Antarctica.

> "Going to a local travel agency they had one tour of Antarctica to offer. Dodson asked if he could explore areas by himself and was promptly told "I'm afraid that won't be possible.""

There seems to be a difference between online reality and real reality.

Article: Newshubnz, 2017, Travel to Antarctica is strictly controlled under the Antarctica Treaty.

> A Norwegian explorer named Jarle Andhoy attempted traveling to the region and was shot at by Chilean ships on one attempt. On other attempts he was intercepted by Naval Vessels from other countries. He has been arrested, fined, denied entry to various waters, and treated like a criminal for wanting to do nothing more than explore the Antarctic.

If the 1959 Treaty says the Antarctic belongs to no one then why are there ships from multiple countries patrolling its waters keeping people out? So it seems we must come to the understanding that concerning this protected place called Antarctica there are two claims that cannot be verified.

1. The scientific world cannot truthfully claim Antarctica is a continent because no independent study can be made to validate this claim.

2. The flat earthers cannot validate their claim that the real Antarctica is an ice wall surrounding the flat earth for that same reason.

So today as the Church looks to science for its answers on how the world was created, the truthseeker cannot count on bible believing Christians to corroborate their own Gods version of what the earth really looks like. Why is it important to understand the biblical reality of a flat earth? Because in the minds of the Christian world, modern science has replaced the location of where God says He dwells with— empty space.

> Isaiah 66: 1, *Thus says the LORD, "Heaven is My throne and the earth is My footstool.*
>
> Isaiah 40: 22, *It is He who sits above the circle of the earth, And its inhabitants are like grasshoppers.*
>
> Acts 7: 49, *'HEAVEN IS MY THRONE, AND EARTH IS THE FOOTSTOOL OF MY FEET; WHAT KIND OF HOUSE WILL YOU BUILD FOR ME?' says the Lord.....*

God is clearly telling us the location of Heaven is just above the firmament that is covering the earth as He looks down on us as grasshoppers. But the Christian believer in the science of man is saying to the world that God didn't create the firmament. That God didn't place the sun, the moon, and the stars in this same firmament. That God didn't stop the sun from moving in the book of Joshua. That Gods earth is not on pillars as He said it was. That even though God said the earth cannot be moved, it is the Christian as a believer in the science of man that will call this claim by God false. The question is placed before you. What kind of house will you build for God if you are a believer in the science of man that has kicked Him off His throne?

John 3: 12, (Jesus says) *If I told you earthly things and you do not believe, how will you believe if I tell you heavenly things?*

CHAPTER ELEVEN

THE TRIBULATION IS OVER AND YOU MISSED IT

Considering the phony plandemic of Covid 19, the current economy tanking, the worlds food supply chain breaking down, the democrats successfully stealing the 2020 and 2022 elections, and now world war brewing in the Ukraine and elsewhere, prophesy hounds are in full throttle as end times revelations manifest in their minds. But did all these guys and gals miss something, somewhere, in the book they use to justify their predictions?

My answer to them is yes, they did miss something. They all got caught up in current world events and began applying them to some biblical quotations that seemed to explain biblical prophesy in a way that fits their narrative. Add this phenomenon to a lifetime of cultural indoctrination by your parents, your friends, your schools, popular culture, and your government, and what you end up with is a conditioned individual socially engineered to look the other way when reality presents itself.

Why this missed reality in question will not qualify for discernment by this individual is explained in two ways:

1. This matter, although real, cannot mentally exist on an individuals radar screen because it has been **long accepted as a non-issue** by themselves and everyone they know so therefore

it is not personally, socially, or culturally, worthy of thought consideration or discernment.
2. This matter in the mind of the individual who is currently experiencing this reality has been given the understanding by a consensus of outside influences that confirmed in his mind **that this matter has been long settled** and therefore it is not personally, socially, or culturally, worthy of thought consideration or discernment.

With this type of conditioning present, the individual will physically look through or past a reality while not mentally registering the existence of what they saw.

It is in Matthew 24, where we will find Jesus prophesying about the coming tribulation. Other gospels referencing the tribulation are in Luke 21, and Mark 13. Since Matthew 24, is the most definitive tribulation prophesy I will reference this gospel.

> Matt. 24: 3, *As He was sitting on the Mount of Olives, the disciples came to Him (Jesus) privately, saying, "Tell us, when will these things happen, and what* will be *the sign of Your coming,* **and of the end of the age?***"*

So the first thing here to understand is we are not looking at the end of the world but at the end of an age. The big question presented to Jesus by the Apostles is: When are these signs predicted by Jesus going to happen? The first hint in the answer by Jesus is "who" is going to be present when it happens.

> Matt. 24: 4, *And Jesus answered and said to them, "See to it that no one misleads* **you***. 5, For many will come in My name, saying, 'I am the Christ,' and will mislead many. 6,* **You** *will be hearing of wars and rumors of wars. See that* **you** *are not frightened, for* those things *must take place, but* that *is not yet the end.*

If you will notice Jesus is telling His disciples that they are the "you" He is talking about and for them "personally" to see to it no one misleads them. And they (the disciples) will be hearing of wars, and that they themselves should not be frightened. What we can understand from this scripture here is Jesus is telling His disciples it is "they" who will be present during this coming event. And what coming event is Jesus warning His disciples about?

> Matt. 24: 9, *"Then they will deliver **you** to **tribulation**, and will kill **you**, and **you** will be hated by all nations because of My name.*

This event is identified as the Tribulation. Jesus is not saying in the future someone will be in the tribulation. He is telling His disciples that it is "they" who will be alive during the tribulation and it is they who will be killed and hated by all nations.

> Matt. 24: 16, *then those who are in Judea must flee to the mountains.*

Is not Judea the ancient southern kingdom of Israel? Is it not true that this kingdom does not exist anymore? So again this tribulation is referencing a time frame when Judea was a functioning kingdom.

> Matt. 24: 25, *Behold, I have told you in advance...*

Told who in advance? If you read the entire prophesy of Matthew 24, you will find it is a current warning of a soon coming tribulation that will personally affect His living disciples. There is no future warning for future people not born yet.

> Matt. 24: 29, *"But immediately after the tribulation of those days THE SUN WILL BE DARKENED, AND THE MOON WILL NOT GIVE ITS LIGHT, AND THE STARS WILL FALL from the sky, and the powers of the heavens will be shaken. 30, And then the sign of the Son of Man will appear in the*

> *sky, and then all the tribes of the earth will mourn, and they will see the SON OF MAN COMING ON THE CLOUDS OF THE SKY with power and great glory. 31, And He will send forth His angels with A GREAT TRUMPET and THEY WILL GATHER TOGETHER His elect from the four winds, from one end of the sky to the other.*

Here Christ is telling His disciples that some of them will see the end of the tribulation. So in verse 29 – 31, the tribulation is said by the bible to have ended with Jesus's second coming. Not a far away future event but this happens also during His disciples lifetimes.

> Matt. 24: 32, *"Now learn the parable from the fig tree: when its branch has already become tender and puts forth its leaves, you know that summer is near; 33, so, you too, when you see all these things, recognize that He is near,* right *at the door.* 34, **Truly I say to you, "this generation" will not pass away until "all" these things take place.** 35, *Heaven and earth will pass away, but My words will not pass away.*

> Luke 21: 32, *Truly I say to you, "this generation" will not pass away until all things take place.*

> Mark 13: 30, *Truly I say to you, "this generation" will not pass away until all these things take place.*

Is there anything left to your imagination as to when the tribulation will happen? Jesus tells us again His disciples will see "all" these things He has just told them about during the tribulation. Then to cap this off Jesus says "this generation" will not pass away until "all" these things take place. This generation clearly means the generation that is currently alive during the time period Jesus was alive and it is that specific generation who will be the ones experiencing the tribulation. The language in Luke 21, and Mark 13, also reveal the tribulations time period during the disciples lives as referenced in Matthew. So can the bible say it any clearer?

The tribulation happened during the generation of Christs disciples and it was they who would also witness the second coming of Christ as referenced in Matt. 24: 29 – 31.

In Revelations, John tells us he was alive during the tribulation and he also referenced the coming kingdom of Christ.

> Rev. 1: 9, *I, John, your brother and fellow partaker in the tribulation.*

> Rev. 1: 7, *BEHOLD, HE IS COMING WITH THE CLOUDS, and every eye will see Him, even those who pierced Him; and all the tribes of the earth will mourn over Him.*
> *So it is to be. Amen.*

Notice that John is telling us that even the Roman soldiers who pierced Christ with a spear will see Jesus's second coming. That tells us again the time frame for the tribulation was during Christs disciples lifetimes.

With Matthew, Mark Luke, John, and Jesus Himself all in agreement that the tribulation happened in the generation that the apostles lived in, what makes todays prophesy experts believe that this same biblical tribulation is going to happen in our future?

As the Christian world looks hither and thither for some kind of antichrist in these so called last days it is important to understand what the bible says about him or them.

> 1 John 2: 18, *Children, it is the last hour; and just as you heard that **antichrist** is coming, even now **many antichrists** have appeared; from this we know that it is the last hour.*

> 1 John 2: 22, *Who is the liar but the one who denies that Jesus is the Christ? This is the **antichrist**, the one who denies the Father and the Son.*

1 John 4: 3, *and every spirit that does not confess Jesus is not from God; this is the* **spirit of the antichrist,** *of which you have heard that it is coming, and* ***now it is already in the world.***

2 John 1: 7, *For many deceivers have gone out into the world, those who do not acknowledge Jesus Christ* as *coming in the flesh. This is the deceiver and the* **antichrist**.

The term "antichrist" is used 5 times in the bible and only in the epistles 1 John and 2 John. What we can understand from 1 and 2 John, is what an antichrist is, that there are more than one, and that the antichrist was alive and kicking when John wrote his epistles. When the apostles wrote about the tribulation in Matthew 24, Luke 21, Mark 13, and Rev. 1, there was no mention of an antichrist. We know 1st and 2nd John mentions the antichrist, but in the four gospels there is no mention of an antichrist, so it is obvious these two epistles by John were written during a different time period than when Matthew 24 was written.

Even the book of Daniel 12, gets in the act of describing a tribulation type of event as mentioned by Jesus in Matt. 24: 15, but again no mention of such an antichrist in this scripture. So why today do Christians pin an antichrist to the tribulation? The question arises. If the antichrist wasn't around during the tribulation, just who was responsible for such death and destruction on earth during the apostles tribulation?

The reigning pagan power during Christs time was Rome and its emperor was none other than a man called Nero.

Nero Claudius Caesar Augustus Germanicus. The emperor of Rome.
Born: 12/15/37 AD
Died: 6/9/68 AD
He reigned from 54 AD to his death by suicide in 68 AD.

The atrocities committed by this guy were infamous and unequaled in history.

- He is said to have poisoned his wife's father after banishing her then executing her.
- He killed his second wife by either poisoning her or kicking her in the stomach while pregnant.
- He had his young boy lover castrated.
- His next wife was a man that took on the role of a woman.
- According to Suetonius, Nero murdered his parents, wife, brother, aunt, and many others close to him.
- Church Father Eusebius notes that Nero was the first emperor who showed himself an enemy of the divine religion.
- Roman Naturalist Pliny the Elder, described Nero as the destroyer of the human race and the poison of the world.

Nero's persecutions of Christians began in 64 AD. This was the first systematic slaughter of Christians sponsored by a Roman Emperor. This story starts with a fire in Rome that many Romans believed Nero to be the one responsible because it was he who wanted to rebuild in that same location the fire was set. To deflect blame from himself Nero declared that the fire was started by a small Christian community in Rome. He had the Christians arrested and began to put them to death in the most horrific of ways and many of them for the amusement of the citizens of Rome. These persecutions included covering them with animal skins and having them torn apart by dogs. They were forced to face gladiators in the arena. They were eaten by lions. They were nailed to crosses and others were tied to poles and lit on fire to illuminate Nero's gardens at night. The apostle Paul was tortured and beheaded by Nero. The apostle Peter was crucified upside down on an X shaped cross by Nero.

When word got out of Rome's persecutions of Christians these atrocities then spread throughout other parts of the empire. This was the tribulation Christ warned His apostles about. Since we know there is no mention of an antichrist we have John who tells us he was in the tribulation and it is he who described the beast of revelation.

> Rev. 13: 11, *Then I saw another beast coming up out of the earth; and he had two horns like a lamb and he spoke as a dragon.* 12, *He exercises all the authority of the first beast in his presence. And he makes the earth and those who dwell in it to worship the first beast, whose fatal wound was healed.*

This first beast is Nero.

> Rev. 13: 15, *And it was given to him to give breath to the image of the beast, so that the image of the beast would even speak and cause as many as do not worship the image of the beast to be killed.* 16, *And he causes all, the small and the great, and the rich and the poor, and the free men and the slaves, to be given a mark on their right hand or on their forehead,* 17, *and* he provides *that no one will be able to buy or to sell, except the one who has the mark,* either *the name of the beast or the number of his name.*

> Rev. 13: 18, *Here is wisdom. Let him who has understanding calculate the number of the beast, for the number is that of a man; and his number is six hundred and sixty-six.*

This 666 number is not a computer chip but a language coded number of a man that John knew about. The Hebrew spelling of: "Nero Caesar" is: NRWN QSR. Using the gematria code for the numeric equivalent of Nero's name we arrive at:

N = 50
R = 200
W = 6
N = 50
Q = 100

S = 60
R = 200
= 666

Article:https://www.agapebiblestudy.com/charts/Gemetria%20and%20 the%20Number%20of%20the%20Beast%20666.htm

> "John warns us that to solve this puzzle takes shrewdness and cleverness! The Roman Emperor we know as Nero Caesar had two common spelling for his name in the first century. One form was Nero Kesar but the Hebrew spelling is Neron Kesar. If you add up the letter values in Hebrew (that's why it takes shrewdness–most people did not know Hebrew) Nero Caesar (Neron Kaisar) adds up to 666. Neron Kaisar = **Nrwn Qsr** in Hebrew which used no vowels, was the linguistically correct Hebrew form of spelling Nero's name.

It was Nero, the first beast of revelations that was identified in the coded gematria code 666 that John warned us about so long ago. The beast emperor of the tribulation. So armed with the understanding that the tribulation is long past, we understand that it is the apostles who were not only going to experience this tribulation but also witness the second coming of Christs kingdom here on earth.

1. Christ warns his disciples of a coming tribulation during their life time.
2. Nero, the beast of tribulation persecutes the Christians.
3. The tribulation ends and Christ's 2nd coming brings His kingdom down to earth.

Christ gives us the timing of His second coming.

> Matt. 24: 29, *"**But "immediately" after the tribulation** of those days THE SUN WILL BE DARKENED, AND THE MOON WILL NOT GIVE ITS LIGHT, AND THE STARS*

> *WILL FALL from the sky, and the powers of the heavens will be shaken.* 30, *And **then the sign of the Son of Man will appear in the sky**, and then all the tribes of the earth will mourn, and **they will see the SON OF MAN COMING ON THE CLOUDS OF THE SKY with power and great glory**.* 31, *And He will send forth His angels with A GREAT TRUMPET and THEY WILL GATHER TOGETHER His elect from the four winds, from one end of the sky to the other.*

This event in Matthew 24 and Revelations 19, is the second coming of Christ right after the tribulation ended and Jesus is coming to conquer Nero's armies and the world. But here again Christ tells us that some of His apostles will be there to witness His 2nd coming kingdom.

> Matt. 16: 28, *"Truly I say to you, there are some of those who are standing here who will not taste death until they see the Son of Man coming in His kingdom."*

> Mark 9: 1, *And Jesus was saying to them, "Truly I say to you, there are some of those who are standing here who will not taste death until they see the kingdom of God after it has come with power."*

> Luke: 9: 27, *"But I say to you truthfully, there are some of those standing here who will not taste death until they see the kingdom of God."*

Another consensus between Matthew, Mark, and Luke. As we remember it was also recorded in these three same books that Jesus told them that the tribulation would happen during these same apostles generation.

It is John who tells us what Christs 2nd coming victory looked like.

> Rev. 19: 11, *And I saw heaven opened, and behold, a white horse, and He who sat on it* is *called Faithful and True, and*

in righteousness He judges and wages war. 12, *His eyes* are *a flame of fire, and on His head* are *many diadems; and He has a name written* on Him *which no one knows except Himself.* 13, *He is clothed with a robe dipped in blood, and His name is called The Word of God.* 14, *And the armies which are in heaven, clothed in fine linen, white* and *clean, were following Him on white horses.* 15, *From His mouth comes a sharp sword, so that with it He may strike down the nations, and He will rule them with a rod of iron; and He treads the wine press of the fierce wrath of God, the Almighty.* 16, *And on His robe and on His thigh He has a name written, "KING OF KINGS, AND LORD OF LORDS."*

Rev. 19: 19, *And I* **saw** *the beast* (Nero) *and the kings of the earth and their armies assembled to make war against Him who sat on the horse and against His army* 20, *And the beast* **was** *seized, and with him the false prophet (the second beast) who performed the signs in his presence, by which he deceived those who* **had** *received the mark of the beast and those who worshiped his image; these two* **were** *thrown alive into the lake of fire which burns with brimstone.* 21, *And the rest* **were** *killed with the sword which came from the mouth of Him who sat on the horse, and all the birds* **were** *filled with their flesh.*

You will notice the language in these verses are in the past tense as they describe this event that happened long ago but after the tribulation. With the tribulation over and Christs victory completed and His kingdom brought down to earth at His second coming, here is the next biblical event.

Rev. 20: 1, *Then I saw an angel coming down from heaven, holding the key of the abyss and a great chain in his hand.* 2, *And he laid hold of the dragon, the serpent of old, who is the devil and Satan, and bound him for a thousand years;* 3, *and*

> he threw him into the abyss, and shut it and sealed it over him, so that he would not deceive the nations any longer, until the thousand years were completed; after these things he must be released for a short time.

> Rev. 20: 4, *Then I saw thrones, and they sat on them, and judgment was given to them. And I saw the souls of those who had been beheaded because of their testimony of Jesus and because of the word of God, and those who had not worshiped the beast or his image, and had not received the mark on their forehead and on their hand; and they came to life and reigned with Christ for a thousand years.*

What Revelations 20 is telling us in verses 1 thru 7 is:

1. Satan was bound in chains for 1000 years.
2. The victims of the beast system under Nero during the tribulation who did not receive his mark in their foreheads or hands came back to life and reigned with Jesus for 1000 years in His kingdom here on earth.
3. What this means is we as Christians today are living after Christs 1000 year kingdom that WAS already here on earth.
4. Christs kingdom after the 1000 year reign has left the earth.
5. And Satan "now" has been released for a short time to deceive the nations.

Verse 3, tells us Satan is back in business for a short time. How long it is this time?

If Christs 2nd coming reign was 1000 years we can guess a short time is not half that time period. So an educated guess could be approximately 200 to 350 years Satan will be again approximately 200 to 350 years Satan will be again loosed on the earth and we as Christians are living in this time frame today.

So I believe two questions are now at hand.

Question 1: What century are we in now since Christs 1000 year kingdom has come and went?
    a) From Christs birth to His passing. (33 years)
    b) Tribulation. (4 to 10 years?)
    c) Christs war with the beast. (1 year?)
    d) Christs 1000 year reign on earth.
    e) Satan loosed on the world for a short time. (200 – 350 years)

Answer: The approximate time period we are living in "now" is loosely somewhere in the neighborhood of 1300 - 1500 AD. Yes you read that right. It is not the year 2022 and yes again, someone has been lying to you your whole life.

Question 2: If Christs 1000 year kingdom was already here on earth, where is the evidence?
    Answer: Everywhere. But the problem is you have been socially conditioned not to see or question a reality that you have been looking at all your life. To put it in a nutshell.

"You cannot find what your not looking for"

I am going to deal with your social conditioning using this approach:
    A picture is presented to you to look at. It is an old black and white photo of a city somewhere in the 1800's. In this photo you see people walking and horses pulling wagons. Framing this picture are large old ornate buildings.
    Now you are asked: What do you see?
    Well you think to yourself. I see people walking and horses pulling wagons.
    You are then asked: Is that all you see?
    You think again. Well people walking and horses pulling wagons and buildings.
    You are asked again. What is this picture telling you?

But your socially conditioned eyes only see people walking, horses pulling wagons, and big buildings in the background.

Having failed to see what this photo is showing you, you are now asked to take another look and ask yourself during what time period do you think this photo was taken?

Well you think, its probably in the 1800's because their transportation is horses and wagons.

And you are correct. But that is as far as your social conditioning will allow you to go. But someone who is NOT socially conditioned to NOT see what is in front of them, will see is this:

The people in the photo have advanced to the developed stage of horse and wagon technology. If this is as far as their civilization has advanced then just who built those buildings in the photo? The engineering required to build such large buildings and the equipment needed did not exist during that time period. These people had hammers and chisels and basic construction equipment. They didn't have power tools, no computers, no cranes, no bulldozers, no elevators, no electricity, and no gas powered engines. But still there they are. Huge ornate buildings several stories high built by people that the best they could do is ride horses to get around. What is this photo telling you? That these people inherited those buildings from a more advanced civilization. For more proof of this architectural claim we can go even further back in time to witness even more amazing buildings "supposedly" built by people with even less technology.

West Minster Abbey. The Abbey in its current form **was said** to have been built by Henry III, beginning in 1245 and consecrated in 1269.

Cathedral of Triar. **Said to have been** built in the 4th-century, **(said to have been)** expanded over the course of thousands of years.

St. Peters Basilica. St. Peter's Basilica in the Vatican City is by far the most impressive. **Said to be Dating** back to 333 **(said to have been)** rebuilt in the 16th-century.

Bourges Cathedral. In the beginning of the 13th century **(said to have been built)**, this Roman Catholic Cathedral was erected in Bourges, France.

Saint Michel d'Aiguilhe, is the oldest chapel of Le Puy. France. **(said to have)** Built the chapel in 962. The chapel was extended in the 12th century. I guess we are supposed to believe ancient serfs carried all those stones up that rock hill and built this church with their hammers and chisels?

Highclere Castle, England. (said to have been) Built around 1679 in Hampshire, England,

So we are told to believe that these people many centuries ago had the technology to build these huge churches and castles right? Just used their wagons, carts, hammers, saws, ink feather quills, and rocks right? What you are experiencing is your socially engineered mind was convinced by others to accept their explanations given to you on how these buildings came to be. Therefore, you considered the matter settled and not worthy of your discernment. Compared to the square concrete gray buildings of today, these ancient buildings give us the impression a higher civilization was responsible for such architectural masterpieces. What you are looking at is the historical evidence of Christs 1000 year kingdom.

Still not convinced?

Then let us look at modern technology at work. Let us compare todays building architecture with the castles and churches of yesterday.

Miami

New York

Chicago

Boston

Do the modern buildings of today look remotely similar to the buildings of centuries ago? The question should manifest itself. Why did the art of constructing yesterdays architecture not get passed on to todays builders? How come there is no evidence of a documented linear development of the worlds architecture? What you are witnessing is a conceptual disconnect between today and yesterday as evidenced by compared architecture.

If you will notice most of the old churches and castles have some type of a dome or steeple of some kind. These are not just for looks. These were receivers to generate natural power from the earths ether. Many times in the courtyard of these ancient buildings you will find a small square or octagon structure. No longer there and strangely missing, this is where it has been speculated that the ancient generators were that received the energy from the domes and steeples to generate power for the areas buildings. It was Nicola Tesla, the scientist, that was working on this same free energy from the ether in the first half of the 1900's.

There's a story circulating on the internet regarding a world empire lost in the chronicles of history. An empire that once seemed to be world known but is now forgotten and buried in the sands of time. It is believed by some that Christs 1000 year kingdom is that forgotten world empire that was once called "Tartaria" which still can be found on ancient maps but for some reason not discussed in todays halls of higher learning.

This ancient empire of Tartaria is at the center of a conspiracy theory that is growing. Proponents of this theory say there was once an advanced, geographically massive civilization that dominated the Earth's surface called Tartaria. As recently as 300–400 years ago, a flood of mud damaged or destroyed many of their buildings and ever since there's been a cover up going on. But what evidence is there of this supposed empire? Why cover it up? The Capitol in Washington DC, European castles, medieval churches, and the Great Wall of China, are all claimed by some to be remnants of Tartaria. These architectural remnants stand as evidence that a civilization much more advanced than ours once ran the world at one time in history. Other buildings, like Old Penn Station in New York City and the Moir's Chambers in Perth, it is claimed were intentionally destroyed to also hide the Tartarian history.

Was the kingdom of Tartaria Christs 1000 year kingdom? It is an educated guess that it was. But the powers of the world have done much to prevent discussion and study that could further our understanding of this lost empire.

To add to the evidence of Christs kingdom here on earth, if you look at some of the ancient coinage there seems to be an oddity with some of them that just seems to leave some of us wondering.

We are told this coin is a silver proof of an Irish farthing of George II struck in 1737.

1. When looking at this coin one will first check the date to see how old it is.
2. Next one will look at where this coin came from. Hibernia / Ireland.
3. Then one will look at who is on the coin
4. Then one will give the coin a once over for any curiosities that catch your eye.

But your eyes betray you again.

I showed this coin to 5 people and two were coin collectors. All five confirmed their social programming by not seeing the reality of what was directly in front of them.

May I direct your eyes to the date again?

You are not looking at the date 1737. You were programmed to read a date that way so you overlooked the first number which is not the number 1 at all. It is the letter "J". You will even notice the printing of this letter is slightly smaller than the other three numbers. What this coin is telling you is it was minted in the the year 737 AD. This "J" your eyes would not let you see represents non other than Jesus. The year of our Lord Jesus 737. (J 737)

Believe me when I tell you I had one guy repeat to me no less than 3 times that the date was 1737 while looking at this coin each time.

This is a Gunmoney Shilling (they say) issued in May 1690. May I again direct your eyes to look closer at the date said to be 1690. The "1" again is not the number 1 at all. It is also a "J". This coin is representing the year of our Lord "Jesus" in 690. (J 690)

Now I understand a person may have trouble with this claim but for those who are please tell me two things. First, why am I seeing a "J" sitting right where the "1" should be? And second, why is someone telling me that the letter "J" is now the number "1"?

Austria (Hungary, Ladislaus) A Ducat coin **(said to date)** 1590. But turn your eyes again to the date. The number "1" is really the letter "I" and again is shorter than the rest of the numbers. This "I" is for Iesus, which is the Latin spelling for Jesus. (I 590) In Latin, " i " can sometimes behave like a consonant. Typically at the start of a proper noun like Iulius or Iesus. In Latin, that consonantal " i " later became " j " in English.

Italy (Naples) Carlino, Tari, 1/2 and 1 Ducato coin (Charles II) **(said dated)** 1693. Again "i" Latin for Iesus/Jesus. (i 693)

Isn't it odd that all these European countries can create splendidly detailed coins but for some reason cannot get that supposed "1" number to look like the rest of the numbers on the dates of these coins?

A BRIDGE OVER THE SINS OF YOUR FATHERS • 161

Here the powers that be are trying to tell us a coin minted in 693 was really minted in 1693. All these examples of coins are covering up a missing 1000 years.

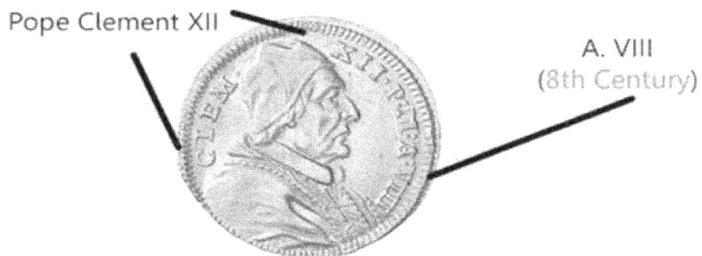

Here we have two popes printed on coins approx. 1000 years before their recorded existence. Now I am not claiming all ancient coins had the letters "I" and "J" substituted for the number 1, but clearly some do and with the addition of these pope coins a thousand years off are we witnessing a 1000 year cover-up? Just who would not want us to know that these coins were minted in the 600's and 700's? Most likely the same crowd that is making sure the lost kingdom of Tartaria remains out of our halls of learning.

For other evidence of the missing 1000 years we see these photos of ancient artifacts.

For some reason the creators of these specific artifacts wanted us to know that this was the year of our Lord in the 600's as evidenced by the "J" put in front of the date.

There are three videos I am going to post here for those who want to take this issue a step further and view parts of this story explained visually.

1. This video is called: The Timeline Deception: Exploring Tartaria, 21 minutes
   https://www.youtube.com/watch?v=Mbfd3BZ_UAY
2. This video is called: Question the narrative: America's lost Civilization, 23 minutes
   https://www.youtube.com/watch?v=IYlA6D-66Ss
3. This video is called: One Day–(Millennial Kingdom Of Christ Already Happened?) 6 minutes
   https://www.youtube.com/watch?v=PdlVRPLf52w&t=1s

So now a question opens up as big as the world itself. Who is behind this conspiracy?

Answer: Look no further than the Catholic Church and the Smithsonian Institute here in America.

The first world international institution was the Catholic Church and they had the financing and the means to acquire most of the buildings leftover from Christs kingdom and turn them into their churches while claiming it was they who built them.

The architecture of these ancient churches is stunning but we are told by the Church that people with hammers, saws, carts, and rocks, built them 500 to 1000 years ago. It was this same Church using their monks rewrote the history of the world as they wished it to be. It wasn't really that hard because most people didn't read back then so they kind of had free reign to create their own version of the literary world. Now would this Church actually have something to hide?

Article: Giants and the alien arrival – the Vatican knows all the secrets! https://mysteriesrunsolved.com/2020/01/giants-and-the-alien-arrival-the-vatican-knows-all-the-secrets.html

Article: Why the Vatican has covered up Humanities pre-flood history. https://www.bibliotecapleyades.net/vatican/esp_vatican199.htm

Article: Seven Dark Secrets Of The Vatican | by Rameen Zeeshan https://search.myway.com/web?p2=%5EHJ%5Expu913%5ETTAB0 2%5EUS&ptb=72257204-043D-4C0C-A9DB-16904A0C993F&n=7 83a0fff&ln=en&si=DSP90&tpr=hpsb&trs=wtt&brwsid=4E610527-1CAF-4FE0-9063-46F00E560DFC&q=hidden+secrets+of+the+cath olic+church&st=tab

While the Catholic Church was busy cleaning up all the left over artifacts and historical information regarding Christs kingdom on a good chunk of the earth, its counter part, the Smithsonian Institute was doing its job here in the States making sure all the traces and trails of that same kingdom was systematically erased from the landscape of our country and the landscape of our minds. But we know the prestigious Smithsonian would never be in the business of covering up history right?

SIDE NOTE: For those who watched the old movie: Raiders of the Lost Ark. The first in the Indiana Jones movie series. In one of the last scenes of the movie we watched a boxed up Ark of the Covenant being wheeled down an aisle in the Smithsonian Institute warehouse then set down in a long row of other boxed up artifacts. If you were looking they were telling.

Article: Did the Smithsonian cover up an Ancient Egyptian Colony in the Grand Canyon? https://sciencevibe.com/2020/02/06/did-the-smithsonian-cover-up-an-ancient-egyptian-colony-in-the-grand-canyon-2/

Aricle: Giant cover up by the Smithsonian Institute–Freak Lore https://search.myway.com/web?o=740311&l=dir&qo=pagination&p2=%5EHJ%5Expu913%5ETTAB02%5EUS&n=783a0fff&ln=en&q=smithsonian%20covers%20up%20american%20history&campaignId=cmpgn-default&qsrc=998&page=3

Article: SMITHSONIAN ADMITS TO DESTRUCTION OF THOUSANDS OF GIANT HUMAN SKELETONS IN EARLY 1900'S https://worldnewsdailyreport.com/smithsonian-admits-to-destruction-of-thousands-of-giant-human-skeletons-in-early-1900s/

So am I the only one who has figured out there is 1000 years missing from our worlds history?

http://www.librarising.com/conspiracy/fakehistory.html
Article: Has our history been faked? "In her goundbreaking work and research, Russian explorer and archaeologist, Sylvie Ivanova, has produced some really eyeopening videos and conclusions concerning our true history. Basically, Ivanova discovered that the further we go back in history, the less accurate our historical assumptions

become. Tartaria, or northern Asia, was the largest and most powerful empire of the Middle Ages, lasting some 1000 years (approx. 500 to 1500AD), with its influence reaching as far as the Americas. It's in all the old maps yet suspiciously missing in the modern ones. *It appears that the Jesuit-led Roman Catholic reformers did a good job at ruthlessly removing all traces of this great empire. Why? Because it was a threat to their existence.* The Tartars were responsible for many if not most of the great structures around the world, from the great churches and cathedrals of Europe (which the Catholics claimed as their own) to the enormous aqueducts both in Europe and Mexico. They also built the Great Wall of China to keep the Chinese out, they built the Coliseum of Rome, the ziggurats and earth mounds, the monolithic structures, the Pyramids, the Serapeum, underground tunnels and more. They left their signature worldwide. All of our dates in ancient history are wrong by 1000 years. "

http://blackbag.gawker.com/is-ancient-history-completely-made-up-by-the-man-1694539419 **Article:** Is Ancient History Completely Made Up By 'The Man'?

Anatoly Timofeyevich Fomenko, a mathematician at Moscow State University and full member of Russia's prestigious Academy of Sciences, has been the leading proponent of a radical revision of human history—"an improved version of the global chronology of the Ancient Time.

Fomenko quotes: The late Russian social critic Alexander Zinoviev provided the foreword to this master work: "The entire history of humanity up until the XVII (17th) century is a forgery of global proportions," he wrote, "a falsification as deliberate as it is universal."

Book: The Lost Millennium: History's Timetables Under Siege
Written by Florin Diacu
Publisher: Knopf Canada
Publication Date: December 2005
ISBN: 0-676-97657-3

A BRIDGE OVER THE SINS OF YOUR FATHERS • 167

The Lost Millennium book explores the astonishing possibility that our calendar is off by a thousand years

Its a comfort to know there are historians today that also have discovered there is a 1000 year missing piece of time when a great empire ruled the world.

So after this historically undocumented 1000 years had passed the bible tells us time was up for Christs kingdom here on earth and Christ picked up His own people and promptly left while leaving us remnants of a superior civilization as evidenced by ancient architecture. So now we today are in that little season. That short biblical time that Satan has been turned loose to **"deceive the nations."** So then does one actually wonder today why so many people cannot see evidence of Christs kingdom here on earth?

For those who are waiting for some sort of rapture I ask you not to confuse Christs historic kingdom that was already here on earth for 1000 years with the thought of some future rapture event yet to come. There really is only two verses that could be used to make the claim of some sort of rapture is on its way. (Rapture: a non biblical word) The rest of the verses assigned to this claim are made up of wishful thinking and theological pole vaulting over biblical reality to defend that narrative.

> 1st verse: 1 Corinthians 15: 51, *Behold, I tell you a mystery; we will not all sleep, but we will all be changed, 52, in a moment, in the twinkling of an eye, at the last trumpet; for the trumpet will sound, and the dead will be raised imperishable, and we will be changed.*

> 2nd verse: 1 Thessalonians 4: 17, *Then we who are alive and remain will be caught up together with them in the clouds to meet the Lord in the air, and so we shall always be with the Lord. 18, Therefore comfort one another with these words.*

It was in 1830 that one John Darby introduced this theological curve ball called the Rapture to the church world. Prior to that year no church ever taught any form of rapture. There is no other way to say this:

"John Darby just thought it up in 1830 and popularized it in 1858 with a group called the Plymouth Brethren Movement."

But what John Darby calls the rapture, the bible calls the 2nd coming.

* To break down these two rapture scriptures, in 1 Corinthians 15, Paul is talking to the Corinthians in Greece – not to the modern day church of today.

* To break down 1 Thessalonians 4, Paul is talking to the brethren in Macedonia and again – not to the modern church of today.

If you will notice in 1 Thessalonians 4, Paul is including himself when he says *"we who are alive and remain will be caught up together with them in a cloud to meet the Lord in the air."* Then he tells them (the Thessalonians – not you) to comfort one another.

Paul is using the same language in 1 Corinthians 15: 51, when he again includes himself when saying: *"Behold, I tell you a mystery; we will not all sleep, but we will all be changed".* You should notice again the use of the term "we" that Paul uses twice in this verse. This statement does not include you a 1000 years later. In both these verses no where is Paul prophesying about some far off future event to a people not born yet. Paul is not talking about the rapture but the 2nd coming of Christ.

Rapture theology is the mother of love theology so prevalent in the modern churches of today. Since God has professed His perfect love for His children, the Christian, smugly immersed in John Darby's invented Rapture theory calmly awaits His exit before things get ugly.

What this invented doctrine does is give the Christian a false sense of security as he believes his loving God would never allow him to experience a tribulation type of event. Therefore a Christians testimony based on John Darby's invented doctrine in 1830 can be easily shattered by a traumatic event.

While God does profess His love for us and wants us to place our hope in Him, that does not change the fact that our creator is a God of laws and has a plan for us that many times is not understood by us. We as His children cannot claim to fully know the mind of God and His thoughts are above ours as He sees the big picture that we do not. Our God given free will means the Christian does not always follow Gods plans for us. This is why God commands us to fear Him because fearing Him means doing Gods will in times of uncertainty while not knowing the future outcome of our current actions.

Today many prophesy experts find similarities in past tribulation events as told in the bible and assign them to our current times. All this means is Satan is up to his old tricks again of deceiving all who will be deceived. Yes there can be wars in our future. Yes there is evil running rampant in the world. Yes the Babylon in Rev. ch. 18, could be an future event. An American future event. And yes the bible tells us in that same chapter there is an incoming asteroid. What else could we expect with Satan on the loose? But if you have opened your hearts and your eyes and have received the understanding that the tribulation has come and gone; that Christs kingdom ruled the earth for 1000 years and now has left; that Satan has been released to deceive the nations for a short time; what next prophesy lies ahead for the faithful Christian?

> Rev. 20: 7, *When the thousand years are completed, Satan will be released from his prison,* 8, *and will come out to deceive the nations which are in the four corners of the earth, Gog and Magog, to gather them together for the war; the number of them is like the sand of the seashore.*
>
> 9, *And they came up on the broad plain of the earth and surrounded the camp of the saints and the beloved city, and fire came down from heaven and devoured them.* 10, *And the devil who deceived them was thrown into the lake of fire and brim-*

stone, where the beast and the false prophet are also; and they will be tormented day and night forever and ever.

Verse 9, tells the discerning Christian of a coming future event.

There will be coming a time in our future when there will be a gathering of the true saints and they will end up going to two places.

1. Somewhere in a camp.
2. In the beloved city.

May God the set the wind at your back, an understanding in your soul, and the strength of a lion in your heart.

CONCLUSION

As the watchmen sound the warning that the church is falling into apostasy, the word of God is no longer revered as sacred. Our shepherds today are more interested in friendship with the world as they preach inclusion with a watered down version of a gospel designed to appeal to the masses.

One day I was talking to some Christians when I asked them a question. "How would you feel about someone who said not all people are not worthy of holy healing? That this same person said some people who were not of his race reminded him of plain old dogs. And that this same guy also said that Christians shouldn't waste their time trying to save everyone." How would you feel about someone like this, I asked them?

The condemnation of this person I just described to them was emotionally unanimous and quick by the Christians I gave this question to. So......would it alter your testimony if you were told it was the Savior who was this person I was just describing?

> Matt. 15: 21, *Jesus went away from there, and withdrew into the district of Tyre and Sidon. 22, And a Canaanite woman from that region came out and* began *to cry out, saying, "Have mercy on me, Lord, Son of David; my daughter is cruelly demon-possessed." 23, But He did not answer her*

> *a word. And His disciples came and implored Him, saying, "Send her away, because she keeps shouting at us."* 24, *But He answered and said, "I was sent only to the lost sheep of the house of Israel."* 25, *But she came and* began *to bow down before Him, saying, "Lord, help me!"* 26, *And He answered and said, "It is not good to take the children's bread and throw it to the dogs.*

> Matt. 7: 6, Do not give what is holy to dogs, and do not throw your pearls before swine, or they will trample them under their feet, and turn and tear you to pieces.

If you were the Christian I told that story to would you recoil in shock like they did when you found out I was describing Jesus? Would you quickly retreat to the safety of the soothing sermons of love from your pastors church? Would you cry out "thats not my Jesus!" Would it then be my place to ask who gave you the authority to create your Jesus?

If Christs words disturb you and cause you in some way to reject His message then you must ask yourself how well do you know your Savior? Are you a bible believer or a church believer? Do you believe in Gods word or your pastors version of Gods word?

Ch. 1: Does it lessen your testimony finding out that we are not all brothers and sisters from the lineage of Adam and Eve?

Ch. 2: Do you feel insulted as a woman or offended as a man knowing that it was a woman who caused the downfall of mankind?

Ch. 3: Do you still believe the flood of Noah was world wide and he and his three sons built the ark and collected all the worlds animals and still were able to secure food for all of them and Noahs family for 150 days?

Ch. 4: Would you still feel comfortable eating pork and lobster?

Ch. 5: Would you now take a stand against the inclusion of the homosexual in your congregation?

Ch. 6: Do you feel a congregation that allows a woman pastor will receive blessings from God?

Ch. 7: Do you still stand with the Catholic Church and support their creation of the Trinity?

Ch. 8: Does knowing God is not everywhere and does not know everything all the time diminish your praise of Him?

Ch. 9: Does it make sense to you now that human graduation into eternity cannot be attained in one life?

Ch. 10: Do you now believe Gods story of creation or his creations version?

Ch. 11: When Jesus told His disciples it was they who would see the tribulation in their lifetimes do you believe Him?

Breaking down walls is never easy. Letting go of thoughts and feelings that have been a comfort and guiding influence throughout your life and can be just as difficult. This can create an imbalance in your life and even a void in your spirituality. But ask yourself a serious question. Was finding our way back to the Lord ever supposed to be easy and comfortable?

> Matt. 7: 13, *Enter through the narrow gate; for the gate is wide and the way is broad that leads to destruction, and there are many who enter through it.* 14, *For the gate is small and the way is narrow that leads to life, and there are few who find it.*

www.ingramcontent.com/pod-product-compliance
Lightning Source LLC
Chambersburg PA
CBHW031630160426
43196CB00006B/357